Mike Pence

with

Charlotte
Pence Bond

Pence, Mike, 1959-
Go Home for Dinner : advice
on how faith makes a family an
2023.
33305255362679
ca   12/06/23

HOME
FOR
DINNER

Advice on How
Faith Makes a Family
and
Family Makes a Life

SIMON & SCHUSTER
New York London Toronto Sydney New Delhi

Simon & Schuster
1230 Avenue of the Americas
New York, NY 10020

Copyright © 2023 by Hoosier Heartland LLC

All rights reserved, including the right to reproduce this book
or portions thereof in any form whatsoever. For information,
address Simon & Schuster Subsidiary Rights Department,
1230 Avenue of the Americas, New York, NY 10020.

First Simon & Schuster hardcover edition November 2023

SIMON & SCHUSTER and colophon are registered
trademarks of Simon & Schuster, Inc.

For information about special discounts for bulk purchases,
please contact Simon & Schuster Special Sales at
1-866-506-1949 or business@simonandschuster.com.

The Simon & Schuster Speakers Bureau can bring authors to
your live event. For more information or to book an event, contact
the Simon & Schuster Speakers Bureau at 1-866-248-3049
or visit our website at www.simonspeakers.com.

Holy Bible, New International Version®, NIV® Copyright ©1973, 1978, 1984,
2011 by Biblica, Inc.® Used by permission. All rights reserved worldwide.

The Holy Bible, English Standard Version. ESV®
Text Edition: 2016. Copyright © 2001 by Crossway Bibles,
a publishing ministry of Good News Publishers.

Manufactured in Canada
Jacket printed in the United States of America

1 3 5 7 9 10 8 6 4 2

Library of Congress Cataloging-in-Publication Data has been applied for.

ISBN 978-1-9821-9036-1
ISBN 978-1-9821-9038-5 (ebook)

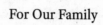

For Our Family

For I have chosen him, so that he will direct his children and his household after him to keep the way of the Lord by doing what is right and just, so that the Lord will bring about for Abraham what he has promised him.

—GENESIS 18:19

GO
HOME
FOR
DINNER

Preface

In the early days of writing my autobiography, *So Help Me God*, I led a delegation of Heritage Foundation supporters to visit historic sites in France. Our trip culminated in a visit to the Normandy American Cemetery and Memorial.[1] It was a cool, cloudy day in Normandy, and one of the men traveling with the group, Price Harding, approached me and made a comment that would stay with me for months. He had heard I was working on a book and wanted to know more about it. When I told him it was a memoir about my life and political career, including the years of the Trump-Pence administration, he was kind and said he thought it would be a success and looked forward to reading it.

Then he paused for a moment and looked at me. "The book I really want to read, though," he said, "is how you and Karen have the family you have with the life you've lived."

I was genuinely humbled by his interest, and, with his observation, came the idea for this book: *Go Home for Dinner*. I am grateful for the positive response to *So Help Me God*, and I felt that there was even more to say—not just about my own career and life but about the family that Karen and I have been blessed with for more than thirty years.

Throughout my life, I've been immensely fortunate. I was raised by wonderful parents, married the woman of my dreams, have three successful children and three beautiful grandchildren, and have had incredible opportunities to serve my country. Through it all, my family's faith has sustained us. Our faith has given rise to timeless principles, ones that have guided our family. I believe they can guide yours, too. They are not unique to us and our story; they are principles common to most successful families I have known. They make it possible to have not only an intact family but one that thrives. I attribute our family's connection and dedication to one another to the grace of God, as well as our humble attempt to live out these core principles. Our commitment to these principles is based on something I believe with all my heart: that faith makes a family and family makes a life.

This book is a modest effort to share our family and our life, to explain the lessons we've learned over the course of our journey that have brought us to where we are today. Although this book includes stories of my family, I hope it is relatable in more general ways. I hope that it reminds you that we all have much in common, that it offers you helpful insights, and that it makes you smile. I pray that the timeless truths put into practice in our little family will be useful for anyone who seeks to balance the challenges of pursuing their dreams and raising a thriving family at the same time.

I'm going to begin with a secret: our culture tells us that "you can have it all," but you can't—not without somebody paying the price. We all have to work, to provide some contribution to the world, but success in work is not the most important thing in life. Psalm 127:2 says, "It is in vain that you rise up early and go late to rest, eating the bread of anxious toil; for he gives to his beloved sleep." I often tell people that if God did not exist, it would be nonsensical to give up your productive time for your family, because it would set you back professionally. But when you make God's priorities your priorities, when you trust Him that family and serving Him are the most important things in life, He will bless you in unexpected ways.

But this book wasn't written in a vacuum. The cultural pressures of the day inform what I've included. I am aware that our country today is not the 1959 America into which I was born. The breakdown of the family is not often addressed in the political arena, but the truth is that the American family is facing hard times. There isn't the popular cultural support for two-parent households or for couples to remain together that there once was. Marriage rates have been going down in recent years as people decide to get married later or avoid it entirely.[2] Social connections and career achievements are given more value than raising successful children and building a marriage that lasts. For those who dream of making family a priority in their adult lives, there are few public models to reference or current examples to cite.

Family vitality, however, is consequential in ways we may not even realize. The steadiness of family life has an impact on the individual level, creating a circle of community on which one can rely. Our families are the primary group to which we are connected. A strong family allows individuals to go through life knowing they have support from their loved ones. But it affects more than our sense of self or our familial relationships; it has an even broader impact. The fate of nations, including this one, ultimately comes down to the strength of the family. Some say that America should come first, but I believe that God should come first, then the family, and then America. But, of course, these are all connected. If you're wondering what you can do to get America on the right track, look first at your connection with the people who live under the same roof as you. Strong faith-based values make strong families, strong families make strong communities, and strong communities make a strong nation.

This is the inside story of one family's lessons, which strengthened us to meet the challenges to come. Wherever we went in life, whatever opportunities were presented to us, my wife, Karen, and I did our best to make our faith and family the priorities. The foundational values we put into practice all came out of the belief that if you put your family first, God will handle the rest.

We have made mistakes along the way, and I will be the first to say that I am not the perfect father nor am I the perfect husband, but these timeless truths strengthened our family, and I believe they will strengthen yours. It's difficult to choose your family when social pressures and enticing career advancements provide more immediate positive feedback. But I truly believe that living out these ideals creates families that are strong and that can withstand even the most challenging circumstances.

And it all begins when you go home for dinner.

1

Go Home for Dinner

Better is a dinner of herbs where love is.

—PROVERBS 15:17

Shortly after I was elected to serve in Congress from Indiana, members of the press and colleagues would occasionally ask where I saw myself in five years. When I would reply, "Home for dinner," I could tell it wasn't exactly what they were expecting to hear. But that response came from my heart and a lifetime of lessons learned.

If there is one piece of advice I would share with the busy men and women reading this book that made the greatest difference in our family, it's this: go home for dinner.

This lesson has its roots in my childhood. My parents raised four boys and two girls in a little house in the Everroad Park West neighborhood of Columbus, Indiana. The 1960s were a busy time and our lives were scattered but full and rich. In the summer, we kids were always outside, playing in the waters of Haw Creek or riding bikes throughout the neighborhood. With all the activity, there were a few constant patterns we could depend upon as kids. The first was attending church on Sunday. My parents put a tremendous value on faith. We weren't a particularly pious family, but we lived out our Catholic faith: at our house it was Mass on Sunday and grace before dinner, and we were taught to be kind to others.

The dinner table was where we came together to end each day. I remember my mom opening the back door and calling for us to come in from a long day of playing outside. No matter what else was going on, we were required to be at dinner, and each knew where to sit, what tasks were required of us to put the finishing touches on the meal. With my dad at the head of the table and my mom across from him, I saw firsthand the value of being present for family meals. I had a role model to show me how to do it, too. Even in his job as a salesman who traveled throughout Indiana several days out of each week, my dad always made a point to be home for dinner with his family. His days were longer than they would have been had he not come home for dinner with us. And he likely missed out on business opportunities by skipping dinners with customers, but he was always there—and it made a difference.

At our dinner table, children were seen and not heard. My brothers and I knew that if we started kicking one another under the table or whispering to one another, we would be in trouble after the meal was over. We engaged in dinner as a spectator sport and were expected to be on time and well put together, with clean hands and clean clothes. As a young boy, I don't think I perceived those dinners as fun. They were enjoyable because they were consistent and we knew we could depend on them. Even though my mother was from an Irish family, where the tradition around meals was always to have more than enough, that wasn't exactly the case in our house. On more than one occasion, I remember looking longingly at the last pork chop left in the middle of the table only to see my dad spear it with a fork and leave me disappointed once again.

It was at that table that I saw what going home for dinner looked like, what it meant in practice to put family above everything else. My parents caught up with each other and smoked cigarettes as the kids observed and learned the values they instilled. If Dad was facing a particularly difficult time in business, he would tell my mother about it, and she would offer him advice. There was often a layer of smoke resting on top of my glass of milk by the end of dinnertime, which had collected as I ate and listened. With no Twitter or text messages, my parents' attention was centered on each other and what was going on in the lives of their family members. Even though my siblings and I weren't an active part of the conversation, the meals still made us feel special because our presence was required—and wanted. For the family dinner to be complete, we needed to be there.

In 1985, I married a beautiful schoolteacher named Karen Whitaker. Karen's parents divorced when she was a little girl, but after her mother remarried years later to a gregarious first-generation Italian American, the dinner table became a focal point of their family as well. Through the example of our families, we had both seen firsthand the benefits of setting aside time every day to reconnect and resolved to share a meal every day. It was a tradition we continued after seeing the birth of three children within four years. Despite our increasingly busy lives, we knew it was an essential part of our family life.

By the early 1990s, I was hosting a radio show syndicated across the State of Indiana from 9:00 a.m. to noon every weekday. It was a call-in talk show to which I brought my Christian, conservative, and Republican values to the news of the day. If

Hoosiers were talking about it, we were talking about it on *The Mike Pence Show*. I had one producer who assisted with the show every day, but beyond that, I had a wide range of responsibilities. I rose early to do all the preparation and host the show. Once I went off the air, I was responsible for working with some eighteen affiliates that carried the program around Indiana and handling most of the sales to advertisers.

In the afternoons after the show was over, I worked in the basement of the modest two-story house that we had bought a few years earlier. We hung fluorescent lights downstairs to create a makeshift office for me, complete with a computer. When you're trying to build something from scratch, it's easy to be consumed by work, hustling to make things happen. Yet even though I was starting a new business, with plenty to keep me busy, I knew I couldn't allow my career to take the place of what mattered most in life. I developed the habit of turning off the computer at 6:00 p.m. and heading upstairs to find one child in a high chair and two others in booster seats at the kitchen table, often with spaghetti sauce smeared everywhere. Because of my upbringing, I knew it was important to be there with Karen and the kids, to get the little ones ready for bed, change their diapers, read them books, and tuck them in with nighttime prayers. Our children needed both of their parents to be a part of their lives, to spend time with them and make memories. The consistent presence of both Karen and me created a stable foundation for their lives.

Once the kids were finally down, Karen and I spent time talking about our day. We didn't want to stop prioritizing time with each other just because we were worn out. It can be hard to focus on your spouse once your kids are in bed and you have a chance to get back to work. Choosing to set aside time for us took intentionality and an understanding that our marriage was the foundation of our family. We knew that if our marriage wasn't strong, our family would suffer as a result. Ending the day catching up with each other made sure we stayed connected through the chaos.

At the time, my going home for dinner didn't involve a commute; I just had to walk upstairs. Even so, sometimes turning off the computer and leaving work behind was the hardest thing for me to do. I like to work and enjoy feeling a sense of accomplishment, but I knew it was more important to end the workday on time and have dinner with my family. It was a conscious decision, something I had to actively choose every day. After all, there's always "one more thing" you can check off your to-do list. Spending time with family in the midst of starting a new business was not only the right thing to do but allowed me to expand what I was able to accomplish. It helped set a precedent of how we behaved as a family. Making that decision when our family was young established a habit that we continued in the years ahead when life was busier in different ways. Hard times will come and there will be challenging moments, but when your family is strong, you can face more—that is, if you choose to go home for dinner.

After I was elected to Congress in November 2000, our life became even more hectic. The life and schedule of a congressional member are often unpredictable, and families rarely move to Washington, DC. But on the advice of friends who had served in Washington, Karen and I decided to move our family to the nation's capital. We wanted me to be a part of our kids' lives every day instead of only on the weekends. I wanted to be home for dinner. Even with late-night votes on Capitol Hill and days full of meetings, I would go home to have dinner with my family whenever I could. That meant skipping the Washington scene of endless receptions and fundraisers. It meant going home in between votes, knowing I would have to head back to the Capitol after spending some time with Karen and the kids. With my family in Washington, I was often pulled in many directions. I would rush home to see the kids before they went to bed, but I was, at times, distracted by the breakneck speed of policymaking in Congress. It meant that I couldn't always debrief my staff on important developments of the day. I often wished I could be in several places at one time, but I knew that my family mattered more than my career. I had to live that out, even when it was difficult. It was all worth it.

Moving our family to Washington, DC, aligned with our larger commitment to coming home for dinner. As a family, we wanted to spend everyday moments with one another rather than see each other only when it fit into the week's schedule. Being around them was also essential for me as I tried to live out my values in the thicket of DC. After spending the day on Capitol Hill—where it's easy for members to start buying into the belief that they are more important than they are—I would walk in the front door of our home to find four people who had absolutely no respect for me whatsoever. My kids have never hesitated to tease me or roll their eyes at my corny Dad jokes. They reminded me that I wasn't as cool as members of Congress are often led to believe. They kept my feet on the ground.

I was also able to be there for my family in a way I wouldn't have been if I had lived in a different state for most of the week. I knew my kids' friends, teachers, and after-school activities. Karen and I had the same circle of friends, too, whether through church, work, or her job at the school our children attended.

Instead of my coming into and out of their lives, we were intertwined. We were a family.

But it wasn't easy; just because we lived in the same city when I was in Congress didn't mean I was automatically going to spend time with Karen and the kids. We still had to put in the effort and make hard choices like every other family. Despite our efforts, there were still times when I didn't make it home for dinner, but because we prioritized time together as a family, we got creative. I have fond memories of Karen and our three children picking up tacos from our favorite spot on the Hill, Tortilla Coast, and meeting me on the steps of the Capitol, where we ate dinner together.

If I had missed lots of dinners, school events, birthday parties, and soccer games, moving our family to DC wouldn't have been worth it. Having them in Washington meant that I constantly had to choose which career functions I would be able to attend. For example, when I was a new congressman, I was given an early opportunity to meet with President George W. Bush at the White House along with other congressional members. But that night, we also had a family event. It was my daughter Charlotte's first violin recital. I had to decide: whether to attend an official meeting with the president of the United States where I could share my thoughts and connect with peers or sit through a squeaky concert of young violinists. I knew all the reasons why I should make the obvious decision and go to the meeting: Charlotte was young, and she wouldn't even remember if I had been at her concert; if I lost my next election because my colleagues didn't take me seriously after I turned down the invitation, it wouldn't be in Charlotte's best interest for me to skip the meeting, either; other members might be given opportunities

I would have gotten if I had been there. But ultimately it was an easy call because of the foundation we had laid as a family. I made it to the recital and sat in the back row in a folding chair as my daughter pulled her bow across the strings of what might as well have been a Stradivarius. She was amazing.

Throughout my political life, there have been other times when I chose not to attend what seemed to be a crucial work event or opportunity that seemed impossible to turn down. It's easy to cave when money, influence, or people pleasing—three things that are abundant in Congress—is on the line. But whenever anyone questioned my decision, I repeated a mantra often heard around the Pence campaign and congressional office. I simply said, "I'd rather lose an election than lose my family."

That wasn't just something the Pence family lived by; we also put it into practice in our office. Our congressional staff was not allowed to stay and work past six o'clock in the evening. We didn't want a workaholic culture—or anyone feeling as though they needed to stay because their coworkers were burning the midnight oil. Years later, Karen continued this in her office as second lady. She encouraged staffers to have lives outside of work so they could spend time with friends and family. Putting loved ones ahead of a job was a standard to which we held ourselves, and we wanted our staff to have rich lives by doing the same.

Finding time to connect with the people who mean the most in our lives is a challenge, and implementing daily schedules that make everybody—bosses, coworkers, friends, and family—happy can seem almost impossible. This is especially true in the world of remote work, where employees can easily feel as if they are always on the clock, even if they are not in the office. Strategies of discovering a "work-life balance" have surfaced to address this very issue. In recent years, it seems as if the concept of "quality time" has grown in popularity as the modern family has become busier and busier. But I actually don't agree with the idea that the quality of time spent together carries more weight than how much time is spent together. When it comes to being with family, I have long believed that *quantity* time is more important than *quality* time.

Today, some people expect to book the time they spend with their children in the same way they fit everything else into their days—by setting aside hours that work best for them. The problem is that kids don't operate that way. Penciling in an hour between seven and eight o'clock in the evening to connect with them is typically not effective. They could be tired after a long day at school, and that could be the exact time they decide to have a meltdown. They could find the cache of Sharpies at six o'clock, and you could be spending the next two hours cleaning up the mess. They might be closed off and unwilling to share when you happen to have a free moment. And we all know that children often switch preferences for parents, meaning that when they want you, they want *only* you.

We have to build consistency and give our children time to open up. I remember countless times when I would ask my teenagers about their day after they got home, to which they would answer, "It was fine." It wouldn't be until later in the evening, often over dinner, that one of them would ask for advice or reveal something that had happened at school. Your children have a desire to connect with you, but you have to create the time and space for that connection to happen. These moments of connection don't always occur when it's convenient. That's why it's important to prioritize not only the big events—such as a violin concert—but also the small moments of connection.

Going home for dinner means sitting around a dinner table, passing food around, and sharing stories about the day whenever possible. For some people, this might not be realistic every night. Not everyone can have dinner with their family because of work shifts, military deployments, or health issues that supersede setting aside time to sit down and have dinner together. When it isn't possible to share a meal, find other ways to sit down and connect with your family. Researchers have found that even having a different meal together during the day—such as breakfast—can be an effective work-around.[1]

Being "home for dinner" is more than just eating together. It means being present in the lives of family members and making a conscious effort not to be distracted when you are with them. Nothing can replace moments spent together and there is little in the life of a family that is more important. Making the time to be with one another, to talk, and to listen can make all the difference.

The Bible says, "Therefore do not worry about tomorrow, for tomorrow will worry about itself" (Matthew 6:34). So leave tomorrow's work for tomorrow. Make your family your priority today. Go home for dinner.

2

Be a Parent Who Listens

You shall teach them diligently to your children, and shall talk of them when you sit in your house, and when you walk by the way, and when you lie down, and when you rise.

—DEUTERONOMY 6:7

Throughout my childhood and young adult years, my mom and dad seemed to be constantly moving forward. They took every opportunity to make sure their kids had full lives, worked hard, and learned the important lessons. It was a given that family came first. If there was a conflict between spending time with friends or family members, my siblings and I knew that family was the priority. That was the expectation, and my parents returned it by putting us first, too.

One of the main ways they did this was by listening to their children. But each of them had a unique way of doing so, proving how parents with different personalities and styles can effectively listen to their children in meaningful ways.

My dad was the kind of father I wanted to be and pray I have been. He worked hard, made his own way in the world, and provided for a family that he raised with an intentionality and purpose that I have tried to emulate. He and I were known to hash out our disagreements, but we respected each other. He didn't hesitate to share his thoughts, and he valued honesty, believing it would ultimately serve us well if he told us the truth, even when it was hard to hear.

For example, when we were growing up, one of my brothers had an especially high opinion of himself when it came to a particular sport he played. Where other parents would have been encouraging, Dad sat him down and told him he wasn't as good as he thought he was. He wanted to tell my brother that before somebody else came along and let him know in a less generous way. Dad was very protective of us, but he would always give it to us straight.

My mother is a redheaded first-generation Irish American girl from the big city of Chicago who also valued listening to her children. Dad was always willing to hear us out and offer advice, but the interest in the minor details that my mom showed was a great blessing to me as a child and later as an adult. When I got home from school in the afternoons while growing up, she would ask me about my day and really want to know everything. That was different from our family dinner table, because during dinner, we were taught to remember our place and give the adults time to talk. But one-on-one, my mom was always quick to listen.

My mom also believed that people learn from their mistakes. If one of her children was hurt, it would break her heart. She wanted to protect us, but she knew she shouldn't always intervene. She had the opinion that there is only so much parenting one can do, and once children are grown, they must learn how to fix their own problems. My mother was always ready to listen, but she didn't want to solve all of our issues for us. And her loving nature didn't extend to letting me wallow in life's difficulties. My mother is relentless in love, but she is impatient with pity.

After I left home to attend Hanover College, I often told people that my mom had a "hot pot of perspective" on the stove waiting for me every time I went home for a visit. Though she was intensely curious about my life and would listen to almost anything, there was one thing she would not entertain: she wouldn't listen to me complain about how badly things were going for me. She had no time for complaints. If I started describing how hard something was or how discouraged I was feeling, she only wanted to know what was next and what I was going to do about it. She had an Irish stoicism that left no room for self-pity. She wanted me to believe in myself and stick to the task at hand, no matter how difficult it might be. Her indomitable spirit always left me feeling encouraged. Even as an adult, when I would head back to work after a conversation with her, I had a newfound sense of strength because I had spent time with someone who knew me, listened to me, and believed in me. I could feel it. It showed. There's really no substitute for that. And with her at ninety years young, it's still true today.

In Congress, I called home almost every Sunday to catch up with her. When I served as governor of Indiana and later as vice president, my calls to her continued. I wanted to hear her thoughts on the week's news, and she never hesitated to share her opinion on how I was handling a situation. But first she listened.

And I listened to her. But the reason I was willing to do so was because of the foundation of love she had established throughout my life.

Listening to our kids is not only an essential part of parenting but you cannot have a strong family without it. And it doesn't happen automatically. Asking, listening, and providing advice take time. They involve fully being there—not just partially or when it's easy. And there are certainly times when doing so is hard. As a father, I've had many conversations with my children where we didn't agree. Those conversations were difficult for both sides. In those moments, I have had to come to the table and patiently hear them out while they voiced their concerns. I've learned that the most important thing I can do is let them know that I take their opinions seriously and want to understand their point of view.

The example my parents set for me by putting their family first and taking the time to invest in their kids' lives set me up for success in my own family. As a father and husband, I am far from perfect. However, being home for dinner was the first step in creating a space where I could be a parent who listens to his children. It provided space for me to hear what my kids were going through, understand the questions and dilemmas they were facing, and know the details of their days. It was a known factor for them—that I would be there and that if I wasn't, I wanted to be.

When you spend time with your children, make sure you invest in their concerns, questions, and dreams—even when you don't see the world the same way. Be a parent who listens.

3

Fulfill Your Purpose

For I have chosen him, so that he will direct his children and his household after him to keep the way of the Lord by doing what is right and just, so that the Lord will bring about for Abraham what he has promised him.

—GENESIS 18:19

The habits of going home for dinner and being a parent who listens were established years before I entered service in politics, but I didn't always have those convictions. I had to learn how to put my family above everything else. As a young father, I was plagued by questions about what kind of difference I wanted to make in the world and what impact I wanted to have. God gave me answers to my questions, revealing what His purpose was for me and what He was calling me to do.

The year was 1997, and our family had recently started attending church on the south side of Indianapolis at the Community Church of Greenwood. With our three young kids in tow, Karen and I made our way through the double doors of the church and found seats on the edge of the aisle so we could make a quick departure if one of the kids started crying.

I was facing a difficult time in my life. I had grown up with a persistent, burdening belief that I was destined to be of service and make an impact in the world. But I had seen those aspirations consumed in the fire of my own vanity. A few years earlier, I had lost two congressional elections in a row. The campaigns hadn't just ended; they had ended badly. My dreams had come crashing down—and it wasn't because of some negative circumstance or unavoidable problem but because of me and my own mistakes. I engaged in negative personal attacks in the campaigns, which weren't honoring to God and did little to advance the conservative cause, resulting in the consecutive defeats that embarrassed me and left me in a place of questioning. The big goals I had always thought I would achieve in life had suddenly come to a screeching halt. It looked as though the career I had wanted and thought I would be good at was gone forever.

Ever since my boyhood, I had dreamed of representing my hometown in Washington, DC, as a member of Congress. I had focused the entirety of my studies on my passion for politics. In high school, I had been active in speech and debate clubs, and I had been good at it, winning national competitions. When I had gone to college, I had studied history under the instruction of dedicated teachers, with whom I would remain in contact for years. I had later decided I wanted to further my education and had gone to law school, where I learned the foundations of our legal system. Every decision I had made in my life had been done so I could chase the dream God had placed in my heart. Yet there I was with that dream utterly dashed.

I was beginning to consider that maybe it was time for me to turn away from the dreams of my youth, grow up, and accept that those ambitions were gone. I had been convinced that God was paving the way for those aspirations to be fulfilled, but I couldn't ignore the fact that doors had not just been shut—they had been slammed in my face.

Along the way, my long-awaited family had arrived, fulfilling years of prayers and patience. In three short years, we had welcomed our son, Michael, and our daughters, Charlotte and Audrey. Our joy in them was boundless, but I still felt as though I was missing out on something. Then everything changed. I found renewed purpose for my life somewhere I wasn't expecting—in those little blinking eyes and a sermon at the church we had just begun to attend.

At the Community Church of Greenwood, we got settled into our seats and the senior pastor, Pastor Charles Lake, arrived at the pulpit to welcome the congregation. He looked like Johnny Carson and had the depth of knowledge and personal touch that made him an excellent teacher and a gifted communicator. He would go on to have a profound effect on my life. Little did I know when I walked through those church doors on that Sunday that Pastor Lake's message would define my philosophy of career, family, and faith for decades to come.

The passage Pastor Lake spoke about that day takes place after God appears to Abraham and tells him that Sarah, Abraham's wife, will have a son. Sarah hears that and laughs, thinking that it can't possibly happen because of their advanced age. The promise has special importance, as Abraham and Sarah do not yet have their own children and desperately want a child. The Lord questions if He should hide from Abraham what He is about to do and says, "Abraham will surely become a great and powerful nation, and all nations on earth will be blessed through him" (Genesis 18:18).

The next verse, however, is the one that changed my way of thinking. It reads:

> *For I have chosen him [Abraham], so that he will di-*
> *rect his children and his household after him to keep*
> *the way of the Lord by doing what is right and just,* so
> that *the Lord will bring about for Abraham what he*
> *has promised him.*[1]
>
> —GENESIS 18:19

The Lord had chosen Abraham, not to journey to the promised land or found the faith, but to "direct his children and his household after him to keep the way of the Lord by doing what is right and just." And the calling came with a promise, that "the Lord will bring about for Abraham what he has promised him."

It was the latter part of that verse that astounded me. Above all else, God was directing Abraham to lead his family. He was calling on Abraham to be a leader in his home. Only through Abraham's commitment to his family would all of the things God promised him come to fruition.

For several years I had been struggling with a lack of purpose, but when I listened to the sermon that day, something moved in my heart. The message opened my eyes and showed me that although God promised that Abraham would have great influence, His instruction to Abraham was that his family came first. His family was his purpose. And I knew from that moment on that it needed to be mine, too.

It was a liberating thought. A warm, comforting feeling washed over me as the weight of what I had been carrying lifted. My perspective shifted. Instead of looking out at the world and anxiously wondering what role I would play in it, I began to focus inward toward my family. My purpose in life was to be a godly husband and father, and if I did that, the Lord would fulfill His purpose for me. God's Word penetrated my heart and mind in new ways of understanding. Suddenly everything clicked: what He wanted me to do right then was put my family first—to love Karen and to lead Michael, Charlotte, and Audrey before I led anyone else.

I had found my purpose; it was to lead and love my family. I needed to see to the members of my own household first and put them above my career, above my aspirations. Getting that right, doing that every day, and making choices to prioritize them is the reason that our family has been able to thrive and do all that God would call us to do.

The sermon gave me a new outlook on life as I realized I didn't have to have every dream fulfilled at that moment. I didn't have to worry about tomorrow. As long as I prioritized being the kind of husband and father that God was calling me to be, the Lord would handle whatever role He wanted me to play in what He was doing in the world. I have read and scratched notes in my Bible for decades. Next to this passage in Genesis are the words "God's promise for me," a note that I wrote to remind myself of the powerful message of that sermon.

And it was true. God's purpose unfolded in our lives. Opportunities emerged, doors opened, and Karen and I would go on to serve our country in ways I never dreamed as I sat in the pews of that church in Greenwood, Indiana.

Perhaps you are like I was in the 1990s and have watched your hopes for the future be shattered. The dreams you felt certain about might have disappeared, and you might be wondering what comes next. I like to think that Abraham and Sarah felt the same way as they entered old age and their dream of becoming parents felt increasingly out of reach. But no matter what you may be going through, there is hope. There is time to build a foundation and to live out principles that will result in the kind of family you want to have and the kind of life you want to live.

First you must come to terms with what your purpose is and choose to live it out. If I may make a humble suggestion: your purpose is leading your family. It is the most important thing you will ever do. Second, trust God to handle the rest.

Once you've decided to lead your family, you can't do it halfway. This central purpose comes with the responsibility of making choices that reinforce it as the most important thing in your life. This isn't easy. Placing one's family and faith above everything else comes at a cost. You will sacrifice time, money, professional opportunities, and a wide network of friends, among other things. Some people will laugh at you, and others will say you will never make it to where you want to go. Some might try to convince you that in order to have influence, your home life is a necessary sacrifice.

For some, it might seem easier to focus on family instead of pursuing service outside the home. I found it to be harder. It was challenging to cede my hopes, dreams, and ambitions, not knowing how they would be fulfilled. And even though family is a smaller stage than public life, I have often had less control in my family than I do in my public life. Maintaining relationships with those closest to you is hard work; being a consistently patient father when your children aren't paid to listen to you isn't easy.

But as I learned, if we focus on our families, God will fulfill the plans He has for our lives. As Genesis predicts, there is a promise on the other side. Put your family first, and God will fulfill your purpose.

4

Embrace Faith

For God so loved the world that he gave his one and only Son, that whoever believes in him shall not perish but have eternal life.

—JOHN 3:16

Since my youth, I struggled with self-confidence. That was mostly because I was the only one in my family with a weight problem. My brothers were active on sports teams and always seemed to be in perfect shape. I, on the other hand, was often shopping in the "husky section" at Sears.

Between my sophomore and junior years of high school, I decided to make a change. I went to see a doctor who put me on a physician's diet, and I started running twice a day. Between Memorial Day and the start of the school year, I lost fifty pounds. When I returned to school in the fall, I was approached by classmates who didn't recognize me and thought I was a new student.

My life was suddenly very different. I attracted more attention from everyone, including young ladies, as I grew in popularity. The success was new to me, and I was flush with confidence. I joined the speech team, where I competed in national competitions, and became involved in school theatrical productions. My newfound activity meant that a lot of people wanted to be my friend. Almost overnight, I had gone from being an overweight guy with few friends to someone who had lots of people who wanted to be around me. My senior year, I was elected class president and was moving up in the world. One of the things that had been holding me back—my weight—was finally gone, and I concluded that I had done it all by myself.

My success in that area led me to doubt the traditions I had been raised in. Catholic faith was a foundational part of our family, but when I began to experience social success, I became convinced that I could do just fine without religion. I saw it as a crutch. It was something that some people—my loved ones included—needed, but not me. I had taken my life by the reins and watched it improve without the help of God—or so I thought.

I gave up on faith in my teenage years, but in our household, going to church wasn't optional. I still attended with my family on Sunday mornings and bowed my head for grace before dinner, but my heart wasn't in it. I had "a form of godliness but [denied] its power" (2 Timothy 3:5). I was simply going through the motions.

As I applied to colleges and ultimately decided to attend Hanover College, my senior year of high school was wrapping up and I was still the big man on campus. I was invited to parties every weekend and was at the center of the social scene. I had reached the pinnacle of my young adult years, and looking around, my fortunes could not have been better. It was confusing to me, then, that for all my popularity and newfound confidence, there was an emptiness in my heart. I couldn't ignore a gnawing sense that something was missing.

At the same time, my oldest brother, Gregory, began attending a Bible study in our neighborhood and read his Bible daily.

I watched as he became interested in theology, which he would go on to study at Loyola University. He began to treat people with more kindness. He had a sense of peace and clarity that I envied. In all ways that mattered, he was a changed man. I was intrigued and wanted to understand what he had discovered.

From time to time, I would sneak his Bible out of his room and read through it, looking to see if I could figure out what he had found in those ancient words. One night, when I was relaxing in the family room in our basement, he walked up to me. "Here's your own," he said as he dropped a Bible onto the couch.

I still have it in my library and will always cherish the fact that my oldest brother gave me my first Bible.

My interest in religion was piqued by my brother's newfound faith, but it wasn't until I went to college that things began to change. I joined the Phi Gamma Delta fraternity, and although I was interested in Greek life mostly for the social scene, I met young men there who described a faith I had never known. They talked about having a personal relationship with God; they explained how God wanted to be involved in every decision I made. I also started attending a fellowship group on campus, although admittedly I went mostly because of the attractive coeds who would inevitably be there. I was engaging with Christianity in a new way, but I hadn't committed to following God.

John Gable was one of the young men I met during that time, and I noticed he was always wearing a small cross around his neck. Wanting to have the same sense of peace and assurance I had witnessed in John's life, I wanted a cross necklace, too, and asked him where I could find one.

"You know, Mike, you've got to wear it in your heart before you wear it around your neck," he said.

His comment stopped me dead in my tracks. John was onto me. I was just trying to fit in and thought I could be a "Christian" by wearing a cross necklace. I was still finding my way to a personal faith.

Before the end of my freshman year, I traveled to a Christian music festival at Asbury University in Wilmore, Kentucky. Between sets, various ministers got up onstage to deliver messages. As I listened to those messages, it was as though I heard for the very first time that "God so loved the world that he gave his one and only Son, that whoever believes in him shall not perish but have eternal life" (John 3:16). With a heart broken with gratitude for what had been done for me on the cross, I stood up, walked down, found a volunteer pastor, and prayed to accept Jesus Christ as my personal Lord and Savior. My life has never been the same.

My faith journey started with my walking away from the faith of my youth, which I had never made my own, and walking down to the festival's stage, where I promised to give my whole life—all my desires, dreams, fears, and hopes—to Him. I was a new man, filled with the conviction that my life was not my own. Jesus Christ had died for me, my sins had been forgiven, and I wanted to live in a way that would serve and honor Him for the rest of my life. I stepped back from the social scene I had grown fond of in my early college days and started voraciously reading the Bible and books about Christianity.

It's easy to think that a path without doubt is ultimately a better faith, but I haven't found that to be true. Had I not experienced doubt and the ensuing disillusionment with personal and social success in high school, had I not embraced my doubts and turned away from religion, I would have never found faith.

My younger years of doubt prepared me for when I had my

own children and they had questions about their own faith. The Bible says, "Train up a child in the way he should go; even when he is old he will not depart from it" (Proverbs 22:6). Karen and I decided early in our marriage that we wanted to share our beliefs on religion and politics with our children but that we would also raise our kids to think for themselves.

That meant, of course, that we had to stay back and watch at times when they went through seasons of doubt and discouragement, which is difficult for a parent to do. Even though the concerned father in me wanted all three of my kids to cling to faith, I learned over the years that they must arrive there on their own. There were times when all I could do was pray for them, but God is faithful, and they each found their way to a personal faith.

My daughter Charlotte has spoken publicly about the importance of doubt in people's walks toward faith. During college, she drifted away from God, and although she never abandoned her beliefs, she would tell you that she wasn't living in a way that honored Him. She wondered if she could avoid the practical habits of Christianity and still be a "Christian," but she soon found that her life was missing something, just as I had felt at her age.

When she studied abroad during her junior year in college, she kept a journal and realized that every time she felt compelled to write something down, a faith component was present. In a moment of deep humility and reconciliation, she had the sensation of being welcomed back into the arms of God. The way she tells it, she realized that while she had been running away from Him, He had been chasing after her. He hadn't left her. As Jesus said, "Suppose one of you has a hundred sheep and loses one of them. Doesn't he leave the ninety-nine in the open country and go after the lost sheep until he finds it? And when he finds it, he joyfully puts it on his shoulders and goes home. Then he calls his friends and neighbors together and says, 'Rejoice with me; I have found my lost sheep'" (Luke 15:4–6). She was the lost sheep, and He had brought her back.

When she came home, Karen and I were delighted to see that new phase of her journey. She was experiencing the Bible stories we had taught her as a child with fresh eyes. As during my experience at the music festival, it was as if she was hearing them for the first time. She read her Bible with a renewed perspective and would often tell us about something she had read with excitement and joy. That experience reminded me that God loves our children even more than we do.

God blessed me with an early experience of the limited fulfillment that comes from success, which would serve me well in the future when more success would come. I'm not here to tell you that success won't fulfill you. It will, but the fulfillment is limited. Once I had a taste of it and decided that I didn't need the "crutch" of religion anymore, I had to face the fact that my life was aimless and devoid of meaning.

Most people go through life operating in the gray area between doubt and belief, never quite embracing either. Henry David Thoreau wrote, "The mass of men lead lives of quiet desperation. What is called resignation is confirmed desperation."[1] If you don't really believe that God is there, admit it to yourself and see how it goes. The questions you have will never be answered if you don't ask them. In my case, asking the questions allowed desperation to be transformed into peace and resignation into conviction.

So embrace faith. But don't fear your doubts—or your children's doubts. They might be exactly what will bring you—and them—home.

5

Sit Awhile with Him Every Day

[Jesus] said to them, "Come with me by yourselves to a quiet place and get some rest."

—MARK 6:31

B efore I graduated from law school, I completed a summer clerkship at the Dutton, Kappes and Overman law firm. It was a high-pressure, competitive environment where law clerks were constantly trying to sharpen their skills and show the partners that they should be hired full-time once they completed their degree. I wasn't alone in wanting to make a good first impression, especially because I also had a lot of personal changes on the horizon. I had recently gotten engaged to the girl of my dreams, and we were planning a wedding. Even though it was a busy time, filled with personal and professional stresses, I had a deep joy that summer and knew it was because of how I started each day.

One day, I walked through the glass doors of the firm and greeted one of the secretaries, an elderly woman, who was sitting behind the desk at the front of the office. I must have been in an upbeat mood, because she commented that I appeared to be doing well.

"Well, when I start my day with His voice," I said, "everybody else's voice sounds different."

She thought about that and said, "I love that."

I've always hung on to the need to start the day in God's Word. I started doing that in college after I accepted Jesus Christ as my personal Lord and Savior. After the music festival, I returned to campus and began to read scripture with renewed eyes. I was born again, and I had a new desire to grow in my faith. The believers who led me to Christ demonstrated the importance of taking time for prayer and reading the Bible. Psalm 119:9 says, "How can a young person stay on the path of purity? By living according to your word." Psalm 119 is the longest psalm in the Bible, and throughout it, there is one singular message, which is a consistent theme throughout scripture: read God's Word. Just read it. You don't have to be a scholar or a theologian or a preacher. Just read it, and God will speak to you through it.

And so I did. It has helped me time and again when I have needed to remember God's calling on my life.

I have had the same One Year Bible for many years. In it, each day of the calendar year includes a psalm, a proverb, and portions from the Old and New Testaments for that day's readings. Beside each of the Bible passages, I have written extensive notes, including in which year I am reading them. I've been able to look back over the years and see what God has done for me or what I was struggling with at any given time. It has become a journal of sorts, a record of how God has been faithful throughout my life.

If you're not sure where to start when you open your Bible, the Psalms are a helpful place to find encouragement and peace. They also have a lot to say about the practice of spending time in scripture. Psalm 19:7–9 says, "The law of the Lord is perfect, refreshing the soul. The statutes of the Lord are trustworthy, making wise the simple. The precepts of the Lord are right, giving joy to the heart. The commands of the Lord are radiant, giving light to the eyes. . . . The decrees of the Lord are firm, and all of them are righteous." I have also found that the psalms honestly discuss suffering and discontentment, even frustration with God. David laments throughout the psalms, and seeing how he—who is described as a man after God's own heart (Acts 13:22)—struggled in his faith has been encouraging to me.

Psalms 1 and 119, the first psalm and the longest one, respectively, also detail the importance of becoming familiar with God's Word:

> Blessed is the one
> who does not walk in step with the wicked
> or stand in the way that sinners take
> or sit in the company of mockers,
> but whose delight is in the law of the Lord,
> and who meditates on his law day and night.
>
> —PSALM 1:1–2

> How can a young person stay on the path of purity?
> By living according to your word.
> I seek you with all my heart;
> do not let me stray from your commands.
> I have hidden your word in my heart
> that I might not sin against you.
>
> —PSALM 119: 9–11

After years of doing our Bible studies individually, Karen and I have started doing our daily devotions together. Even when I'm on the road, I call her to talk through that day's reading. It only took us thirty-eight years of marriage to learn that we should make time every day to read the Bible and pray together. It's a way for us to remain connected and keep our minds grounded when we have to make major decisions. It also allows us to pray for each other and for our family and friends, and to share our concerns and burdens. Before we read through the passages, we pray that God will show us what He wants us to see. And without fail, He does. Karen will often read something that I miss, or I will catch something that pertains to a problem we are facing. It provides us with the answers we are seeking from God and draws us closer to each other in the process.

———

Beginning in law school, in the mornings somewhere between wake and sleep, I began to imagine a recurring scene. In it, I am walking along the side of a tall, leafy hedge when I see an opening in the hedge ahead of me. Peering through the opening, I can see the figure of a man seated on a bench. His feet are in sandals, and He is wearing a robe. One hand is resting on each knee as if He is waiting for a conversation to begin. My heart tells me that it is the Lord who is waiting there, inviting me to pause whatever I am doing and come sit awhile with Him. Beside Him, the bench is always empty. There is always a place for me.

There have been times in my life when I have imagined this scene and the hedge is more grown over than it is at other times. The opening is narrow, and it is hard to see through the leaves, obscuring the person on the bench. Whenever that is the case, it is usually because I haven't been spending time in devotions and prayer. When the hedge is open and the path leading to it is well worn, it is during times when I have been more disciplined about reading my Bible and praying. I can clearly see someone waiting there for me.

So sit awhile with the Lord every day. And if you can, sit awhile with your husband or your wife. Adding another item to your morning list might sound like a chore, but spending uninterrupted time in prayer and devotions will make an immense difference in your life. Not only will it allow you to have a more positive outlook, but it will enable you to hear the still, small voice through the noise. Everyone else's voice will sound different—less harsh and resounding, less important—when you listen to Him. It will allow you to answer the call that He has for your life and to answer others with kindness and see them as people whom He loves, even when it is difficult for you to do so. It will give you the ability to take action and go forward in new ways to impact your family, your community, and the world.

Sit awhile with Him every day. He is always waiting.

6

Talk Faith First

Do not be ashamed of the testimony about our Lord.

—2 TIMOTHY 1:8

After leaving the White House, I spoke at many college campuses across the nation. While I was recently visiting the campus of a Christian college, a student in the audience asked me for dating advice. I thought about it for a moment and told him that he should talk faith first, a lesson I had learned on the way to meeting the girl of my dreams.

As a young man in law school, I started to notice a pattern: Every time I would start dating a girl I was interested in, it would start out well. But when I told them about my faith and how I had given my life to Jesus Christ, the relationship would often cool as the girls' responses ranged from courteous to downright uncomfortable. Sometimes they would say that they also went to church, but when I explained how faith is about more than just going to church, it became clear that our commitment was mismatched.

I started to get frustrated with that cycle, and in the fall of 1983, after my latest dating experience went south, I finally decided to make a change. I had been dating nice girls, but they didn't have the same values that I did, and I realized that arrangement wasn't going to work long term. When I had dedicated my life to Christ, I hadn't given Him just some of my life; I had promised to give Him all of it. I made the decision that I would tell the next girl I asked out about my faith right away. I would tell her at the beginning, even if it created an awkward conversation or meant that our first date would also be our last. I had to put Christ first, and I needed to find someone who felt just as strongly about that as I did.

That very Sunday, my life changed forever. I was visiting a church service with some friends in Indianapolis, Indiana, and noticed a beautiful brunette playing guitar during worship. A few weeks later, there she was again. I gathered the courage to talk to her. That was Karen Whitaker, the most incredible woman I have ever met, who became the greatest blessing of my life.

We started dating, and I stayed true to my commitment. I told her about my faith in Jesus Christ and how I had accepted Him as my personal Lord and Savior. I explained that I had given everything to Him and it had changed my life. I figured that if our relationship wasn't going to go anywhere because of my faith, we should quickly get that out of the way. But she was enthusiastic about my beliefs and wanted to hear more. She had been raised in the Catholic Church, as I had been, and wanted to understand what I had found in a personal relationship with Jesus. When my faith had become real to me in college, I had realized that God cared about all of my problems. That was a new concept to her, but she welcomed it, and our faith grew together.

As we became more serious, we had conversations about the kind of relationship we were building. She once told me that I would always be "number one" in her life, but I told her I didn't want to be that for her. I didn't want to be put on a pedestal, because I would certainly let her down. I told her she would need to make Christ number one and that her relationship with Him would have to come first. If we both prioritized our relationship with God, it would ensure that our marriage was grounded in Him and not based on each other. I knew that making our love the foundation wouldn't hold up once the struggles of life arrived, as they always do.

I often use a triangle as an illustration of this. If both people start at the corners of the triangle and work toward a stronger relationship with God at the top, as they grow closer to God, they grow closer to each other.

It was also important for us to establish the charter for our relationship. For Karen and me, our source of truth was—and is—the Bible. I've always related to the words of Reverend Billy Graham, who once wrote, "I don't understand everything in the Bible. I accept the Bible by faith as the Word of God."[1] Even though the Bible can be difficult to grasp, Karen and I both know it is true, and we based our relationship on its words.

The Bible has a lot to say about marriage, and it explains that God created Eve to be not only Adam's companion but also his helpmate,[2] which in the Hebrew (*ezer*) is the same term used for God in many scenarios when He is helping people. Genesis 2:18 says, "The Lord God said, 'It is not good for the man to be alone. I will make a helper suitable for him.'" We need the help of others, especially our spouses, and I believe that God created marriage not just for companionship and children but so that we would have help always at our side. This help allows us to face the world and achieve God's purpose in our life.

Nine months later, Karen and I were engaged. Nine months after that, I had her by my side. On June 8, 1985, I stood at the end of the aisle in a little Catholic church and watched the most beautiful bride walk toward me. We said the traditional marriage vows at our ceremony, but we also wrote special ones to share only with each other.

Those private promises have been displayed in a frame above our bed throughout our married life. In between the written vows, there is also a symbol. It is an image of a cross with a heart overlapping it in the middle. It reminds us not only to put Christ at the center of our relationship but to place Him at the forefront. Our relationship with Him, as a couple and as individuals, is more important than our relationship with each other. If our relationship with Christ is strong, our marriage will be strong, too. And if our marriage is strong, our family will be, as well.

If you want to have a strong, thriving family, start with your marriage. And when you are looking for a spouse, talk faith first.

7

Go to the Shoot

Do not think of yourself more highly than you ought.

—ROMANS 12:3

When Karen and I were newly married, we lived in the Broad Ripple neighborhood of Indianapolis. It was a busy time for a young attorney and a second-grade schoolteacher, but we were deeply in love and filled with anticipation for the years ahead.

About that time, we heard that a movie was going to be shot at Hinkle Fieldhouse, a sports facility at Butler University, not far from our small rental home. Constructed in 1928, Hinkle Fieldhouse is a National Historic Landmark. It was the largest basketball arena in the country for more than two decades and hosted the Indiana High School Athletic Association's annual basketball championships for more than forty years.[1] It put Indiana onto the map and created a way for fans to attend games and cheer for their favorite teams.

A local radio station began to promote the upcoming shoot and invited members of the public to attend as long as they wore period clothing from the 1950s. We joked about it, laughing with friends about what kind of movie would be shot at Hinkle

Fieldhouse in the middle of Indiana. We figured that it must not be that great of a film if it was being made there and not in a glamorous Hollywood venue. Ultimately, we passed up the opportunity to see it filmed. But the joke was on us.

A few years later, we discovered that the movie was the iconic 1986 film *Hoosiers*, which went on to be widely regarded as the greatest sports movie of all time—and to this day is one of my personal favorites.

The movie is based on the true story of a small-town basketball team in Milan, Indiana, that won the state championship in 1954, making it the smallest school to succeed at that level. The star of the team is based on a real person, Bobby Plump, who secured the title in a jump shot with three seconds left on the clock.[2] The "Mighty Men" of Milan saw a victory that night, and an Indiana legend was born: the "Milan Miracle."[3]

It's a heartwarming story about defying the odds and taking chances on people who are down on their luck. The story of Milan captures the spirit of Indiana. We might be underestimated at times, but Hoosiers show up and often perform better than anyone ever imagined they can. They also believe in their fellow man, even when no one else does.

The creation of the movie is also an underdog story. *Hoosiers* wasn't expected to do well,[4] and Gene Hackman, the actor who played Coach Dale, believed that the film would be a "career killer." But it was actually the opposite; it received two Oscar nominations and raked in $28 million at the box office.[5] It also performed exceptionally well in the home-video market. Most important, it has inspired audiences for decades.

In one of the film's classic moments, Coach Dale and the team arrive at Hinkle Fieldhouse for the championship game. The boys look around at the stadium seats, gazing at the massive auditorium where they will soon have to play, and their nervousness is evident on their faces. Coach Dale asks a few of them to measure the dimensions of the court—the distance from the free throw line to the basketball goal, as well as the rim of the hoop down to the floor. "I think you'll find it's the exact same measurements as our gym back at Hickory," he tells them.[6]

It's an endearing lesson and something I try to remember often in my life. The US Capitol, the Indiana Statehouse, and the White House are all places I have had the privilege to work. For this small-town Indiana kid, arriving in those historic halls often brought with it a healthy sense of trepidation. But when I felt nervous, I would remember that I hadn't gotten there on my own. There's an old saying in Indiana that goes "When you see a box turtle sitting on a fence post, you know one thing for certain: he didn't get there on his own." Anything I have achieved in life is because of the grace of God, my family, and the people of this state and nation. I believe that God has used the opportunities I've been given to prepare me every step of the way.

We all have times when we come across opportunities that seem unimportant, but I've found that it's important to keep an open mind. These chances may well spark our imagination and broaden our idea of what we might achieve in our lives. If you pass on those opportunities, you may miss a moment of inspiration.

Even before the *Hoosiers* shoot, I hadn't learned the same lesson in 1975 when a few high school friends—with a similarly dismissive attitude—skipped a debut concert at the Crump Theatre in Columbus. We were told that the musician was a "new rock sensation" from Seymour, Indiana. We laughed off the possibility that such a lauded musician would be performing in our hometown, and we missed seeing John Cougar Mellen-camp at the outset of his record-setting tour. I should have gone to the concert.

And Karen and I should have gone to the movie shoot.

From those experiences, I learned not to prejudge oppor-tunities when they come along. Not only would they have been once-in-a-lifetime experiences, but only God knows the rich-ness of the experiences we will have. Only He knows why certain people are placed in our path and how we can help one another achieve what His plans are for us. It's important to remember, as the Bible says, that "they do not know the thoughts of the Lord; they do not understand his plan" (Micah 4:12). Just like that box turtle on the fence post, there is more to every story.

So take a chance. And don't dismiss an opportunity out of hand. God might be trying to show you something. You don't want to miss it. Give the concert a shot, and go to the shoot.

8

Have the Faith of a Hummingbird

She is clothed with strength and dignity; she can laugh at the days to come.

—PROVERBS 31:25

While serving as vice president and second lady, Karen and I were asked to pick Secret Service code names. Without missing a beat, she requested "Hummingbird." (I, of course, was "Hoosier.") She loves hummingbirds and has hung feeders in every home we've lived in. The feeders attract the birds to our windows and allow us to catch a glimpse of the speedy animals. But Karen also personifies the spirit and perseverance of those fluttering creatures. In our thirty-eight years of marriage, especially during any hardship and disillusionment we faced, her unrelenting energy has never failed to inspire me.

That became clear to me early in our relationship. When we were first dating, she wanted to return to her first love of teaching in the classroom. No positions were open, and she started to lose hope. I told her that I didn't think God would put the dream of being a teacher into her heart and then not honor it. Despite her disappointment, she never gave up looking for the perfect job. Soon after, a spot at Acton Elementary School in Indianapolis became available for a second-grade teaching position—exactly what she wanted.

Her faith would prove to be resilient during future trials. When Karen and I got married, it seemed that every person in our life was having children. I wanted to be a dad but thought we had plenty of time and kids could wait until later in our lives. My dad seemed to sense that we were wary about starting a family. One day, early in our marriage, as several young grandchildren chased one another around the living room of my parent's home in Columbus, Indiana, my dad smiled and said, "Remember, Michael—there's no good time to have kids. And there's no bad time to have kids." But we were enjoying life, two upwardly mobile young professionals, and we just weren't ready.

Not that we were alone. Americans are increasingly waiting to grow their families.[1] In 2019, more women in their late thirties were having children than they were just a few decades earlier.[2] Similarly, fewer women are having children in their early twenties than did in the past. Like our inclination in the early years of our marriage, couples seem to be waiting for the perfect time. Having children can be a challenge, and I understand the hesitation to start, but I've repeated my dad's advice more times than I can count: "There's no good time to have kids. And there's no bad time to have kids."

When Karen and I decided to start trying to conceive, it didn't take long for us to realize that something was wrong. I felt as though we were hearing about our friends and family members getting pregnant every other week, but months and months went by and nothing happened for us. During that time, a deep and fundamental testing of our faith began as God taught both of us to trust Him with our most cherished treasure, our family, even if it involved frustration and disappointment.

Though not often discussed, the pain of infertility is real. Each year, millions of families in the United States struggle with the disappointment of infertility. It is a silent epidemic of heartbreak.

We scheduled doctors' appointments to find out what was going on. Though no one could explain it to us, Hummingbird never gave up, and we decided to move forward with infertility treatments. Karen underwent gamete intrafallopian transfer (GIFT), which involved getting multiple shots followed by a laparoscopy. Each time, we had to wait and pray that the procedure would be successful.

We told our parents about the fertility treatments. My dad would go to Mass on the mornings Karen underwent the procedures and would stop by our house after to see how she was doing. My world was shattered on April 13, 1988, when my dad suddenly passed away from a heart attack at the age of fifty-eight, but I'll always find comfort in the fact that he knew we were trying to have kids.

Through it all, Karen brought the same steady faith she had about her teaching job to the journey of having children. God gave her the desire to be a mother, and she never lost faith that He would ultimately honor that. She never gave up on our kids. To be honest, though, I did.

By the end of 1990, as we were still struggling to conceive, I was growing accustomed to major disappointments. On top of my dad's death, I had tried and failed twice to launch my political career. Underneath it all, a belief started to set in that things were just not going to work out for us. I was growing accustomed to working hard to achieve something and then watching as it was ripped away from me. Maybe we were one of those couples who simply could not have children. In the words of the song "Higher and Higher," "Disappointment was my closest friend."[3]

Overall, our infertility troubles went on for five years. Karen never stopped believing that God would bring us children of our own, but I was resigned to the fact that He would give us a family in another way. I've always known that He can create families through adoption, and we opened our hearts to pursuing it. We began working with a lawyer and put our name onto an adoption list with a private agency.

I believe that there's no such thing as an unwanted child. There are estimated to be about two million couples waiting to adopt a child;[4] and in 2020, there were almost one million abortions in the United States.[5] During my time serving as governor of Indiana, we worked to make Indiana a pro-adoption state to encourage families to bring children in need of a home into their family. You cannot be pro-life if you are not pro-adoption.

In 1991, five years after we first tried to start a family, I was driving to Fort Wayne, Indiana, for a business trip. I stopped at a gas station to call home and hear the results of the latest procedure. I was ready to comfort Karen and had my words of consolation prepared, as I had so many times before. When she answered the phone, however, her voice was loud and clear. "Happy Father's Day!" she said.

I think people could hear me cheering in the next county. Our joy was inexpressible. It still is.

In the midst of our wonderful news, we received a call from our attorney handling our application for adoption and learned that there was a young girl facing an unplanned pregnancy who was considering selecting us, along with four other couples, to adopt her little boy.

Karen and I prayed about it, wondering if God was calling

us to welcome that child into our family. We decided that we needed more information and asked our attorney to find out if the other choices for adoptive parents were clinically infertile. He learned that three of them were, meaning that they were unable to have children. With a baby on the way, we didn't want to stand in the way of another family having a child, so we withdrew our names.

Trusting God with this pregnancy—the first successful one we had experienced—was an opportunity to surrender our hopes and fears to Him. We had to let go and believe that He was in control. In November 1991, our lives changed forever when our son, Michael Joseph, was born. Even after Michael came into our lives, I spent much of the first year of his life worrying that something would happen to him. It just seemed too good to be true. I had stopped letting myself believe that God would give us this gift after years of longing, and once Michael arrived, I still doubted.

But Karen never wavered. She always believed that God would bring Michael, Charlotte, and Audrey to us. And He did.

———

If there is a small feathered creature nearby, beating its wings and making a sound that resembles a smooth, gentle motor, Karen Sue Pence is the first to know. She will stop what she is doing and say, "Look! A hummingbird!"

There have been seasons when her hummingbird feeders attracted lots of the red-and-green, long-beaked birds and seasons when hardly any showed up. To get a glimpse of these birds and their hunt for nectar is to watch a strategic and persistent dance. Hummingbirds are driven by the search for nectar. They have such high metabolisms that they are constantly in search of food and must feed themselves every fifteen to twenty minutes. Their flight is not one taken for pleasure. Rather, they are on a mission.

I think this is a beautiful metaphor for the way Karen's faith sustained us during the difficult seasons of our life. She never gave up and remained undeterred even in the face of doubt, disappointment, and struggle. Her energy seemed boundless, but it was powered by her faith in God and His promises. Have the faith of Hummingbird.

9

Build the House You'll Need Tomorrow

By wisdom a house is built, and through understanding it is established.

—PROVERBS 24:3

I have often thought that once I get to Glory, if we are permitted to visit times and places in our lives, I know where my heart will take me. I will go back to 1995, to the redbrick house with green shutters that Karen and I built on Inisheer Court in Indianapolis, to the driveway where my three young children would come running to greet me when I arrived home from work. We didn't start out in that house and it isn't where we ended up, but I remember those times with deep joy because of the tender memories with family and because we had to push ourselves to get there.

When Karen and I were newlyweds, we rented a one-bedroom bungalow in the Broad Ripple neighborhood of Indianapolis. As our careers in law and teaching moved forward, we bought our first house in the same neighborhood, a little brick bungalow on Evanston Avenue. We knew we would outgrow it, and we eventually did. Once our children arrived and I began my career in radio, we decided to build our dream home. We thought we were building the house our kids would grow up in and the one in which we would grow old together.

I told my brother Gregory about our plans, and he relayed to me a conversation he'd had with our dad before he'd passed away six years earlier. When Gregory had been considering building a home, Dad had told him, "Don't build the house you need today, build the house you'll need tomorrow." His advice was to build the house Gregory would need in the future, even if it meant he had to push himself to get there, to stretch his resources and imagine where he could go.

I thought a lot about that. We were planning to break ground on a modest three-bedroom home, but my dad's words resonated with me. If we built the house we needed during that time in our lives, we might get too comfortable. We might not take chances on opportunities that would come our way because we were content in the safe life we had created. We decided to take Dad's advice and started drawing up new plans—not for a three-bedroom but for a five-bedroom home, where I could use one of the bedrooms above the garage as an office. The basement would remain unfinished so our children could run and play in it while they were young, and later on we could decide how best to use it. We selected a plot in a new subdivision that was being constructed at the top of a rare standalone hill. We would later nickname the neighborhood "Son Mountain" after a Christian children's TV series our kids enjoyed.

We didn't overextend ourselves, and we weren't irresponsible with our money. We knew we could afford the house, but it would require me to work hard. At the time, Karen was a stay-at-home mom. I had just started a career hosting a syndicated

radio show across southern Indiana. We could make the payments, but I would have to be intentional about going to the office every day with an entrepreneurial drive. I would have to sell
enough advertisements to make the radio show profitable. If we
had built the house with lower mortgage payments, I probably
wouldn't have been as motivated.

Of course, buying a home with payments that push your
comfort zone isn't for everyone. It might not even be financially feasible. But we can all make decisions in our lives that
will stretch us. In my own life, I've found it important to have to
aim at big goals, ones that are loftier than the ones I can easily
achieve. They've kept me motivated and better for it.

We took great interest in every aspect of the construction
of our new home. I have many happy memories of loading our
kids into the minivan and driving over to the construction site
on Inisheer Court. One afternoon, we had the kids press their
hands into the wet cement as the driveway was being laid. We
thought we'd live there forever, and we didn't realize we were
leaving our mark on a home to which we would say goodbye in
a few short years when God called us into politics.

In 1995, during our first Christmas morning in the new
house, our three small children gathered on the floor of the living room. They were bouncing with excitement as they waited
to open their presents. Michael was four years old, and Charlotte and Audrey weren't far behind—at two and one. A thick,
heavy snowfall started. It looked like one of those old Christmas
specials on TV. The sound of crackling wood came from the
fireplace, and the two windows we had designed to go on either side of it were filled with the image of gently falling snow. I
said a quiet prayer, thanking God that we hadn't built the house

that fit us for the moment, and instead had built a house for tomorrow. Our family was enjoying a beautiful time. Change was coming, but I felt peace that we were right where we were supposed to be at that time in our lives.

The Bible describes faith as "confidence in what we hope for and assurance about what we do not see" (Hebrews 11:1). We took a chance, and God provided. We aspired to do more in our lives, and if we had built the house we needed at that time, it might not have pushed us to branch out and trust God in other areas.

As we made plans to move home to Indiana after the 2020 election, Karen and I came across that Inisheer Court house. It was for sale. But we didn't tour it. Thirty years before, we had built the house for tomorrow, and returning to Indiana, we needed to do that again. Karen and I considered buying a small home, but we decided that a bigger place—one that would fit our three adult children, their spouses, and our grandkids—was a better fit. We wanted our family to know that they always have a place to call home.

Several years ago, before it was on sale, we paid the Inisheer Court home a visit. We asked the new owners if we could see the handprints, which were still there right where we had left them, the name of each child still legible underneath the outline of their tiny hands. Michael, Charlotte, and Audrey were teenagers by then, and they humored their parents by placing their hands over the handprints, their fingers spilling over the sides and obscuring the impressions from the past.

Though I may at times remember those early years with longing, at the end of the day, I'm glad our children outgrew those handprints. I'm glad we outgrew that house. I'm grateful that we built a house for tomorrow because it inspired us to dream the bigger dreams that brought us to today.

So take a step in an uncomfortable direction and believe that God will bless your family, your career, and your finances.

Build the house you'll need tomorrow.

10

Know You Are Never Better

Be very careful, then, how you live—not as unwise but as wise, making the most of every opportunity.

—EPHESIANS 5:15-16

Whenever people ask me how I am doing on any given day, I always answer with the same few words: "Never better."

When they invariably express surprise, I explain that I say I am "never better" for a simple reason: since there is nothing I can do about yesterday and tomorrow has not yet come, I am "never better" than I am right now—because right now I can do something about my life and the lives of others. The here and now, this minute, is always the best time to take action. In fact, it is the only time we can do so. That's why I am never better than I am right now.

In the 1990s, I read *The 7 Habits of Highly Effective People*.[1] Stephen R. Covey's message of being willing to act in the moment and seize every opportunity resonated with me. Many people live in a reactionary mode, pushed and pulled by life's events. When we are proactive, we take steps in the present moment that determine our future. As President Theodore Roosevelt once said, "Get action. Seize the moment. Man was never intended to become an oyster."[2] Yet being proactive and knowing what action to take isn't always easy. It means listening to the dreams that God places in your heart and finding the courage to step out and reach for them. There is never a better time to do it.

In 1993, I was named president of the think tank Indiana Policy Review Foundation, when I decided that I needed to launch out on my own and take a risk. I knew nothing about the media business, but I had a dream of starting my own radio show, and I wanted to go for it.

I could easily have stayed in my current job, but I had grown restless and it showed. I wanted to make more of an impact, so I went to the board at the think tank and laid out a list of things I thought they should be doing. They were kind, heard me out, and then wholeheartedly disagreed with every one of my points. I believed that the think tank should be more active in policy debates and talk about the state's issues; I created a plan that included holding press conferences and rallying support behind conservative initiatives at the Statehouse. But the board wanted to stick to a more traditional route when it came to the policy publication. There was no correct answer, and they ultimately had the right to decide what direction they wanted to go in. But I realized then that my remaining time there would be brief. Even though we didn't share the same vision for the future of the think tank, they invited me to stay. It was tempting. We had two kids in diapers at the time, and Karen was staying home with our kids until they were in school. Even though it made sense to keep my steady job and delay chasing my dreams, I felt the pull to be more of a voice in politics.

In the early years of my career, I developed a love of working in radio and saw firsthand how effective it was for discussing politics. In between my early campaigns for Congress, I was invited to host a half-hour weekday show called *Washington Update with Mike Pence* at WRCR radio station in Rushville, Indiana. I would drive over from the law firm where I was working and be on the air for thirty minutes each day. The people in charge of the station were supportive of my political career and helped me stay relevant in between my runs for office. That way, even when I wasn't a candidate, I could continue to improve my name recognition by speaking directly to my fellow Hoosiers. While I was at the think tank, I also became a regular guest on radio and television shows in the state debating state policy issues. I had also been approached about hosting a radio show that would air on Saturdays, an opportunity that I gladly accepted. Without even trying, I had caught the radio bug.

One Saturday in the winter months of 1993, while I was still at Indiana Policy Review, I drove to the station to host the weekend show. I had essentially decided to turn in my resignation at the think tank. But I hadn't made the final call yet. Sitting behind the microphone and speaking to Hoosiers on the air—whether they were in the car driving their kids to sports games or out on a tractor under the Indiana sun—I realized that I was much more fulfilled in that little studio one day a week than I was each day in my job with the policy group. I had enjoyed working there and being part of the political debate, but I wanted to be more involved in the conversation. I wanted to discuss the news with my fellow Hoosiers rather than just inform legislation at the state level.

It was the early days of talk radio, and Rush Limbaugh had hit the airwaves in a sensational way. His show touched the hearts and minds of people all across America. And it gave me an idea: What if I started a radio show during the week that would air before Limbaugh's show?

It was a crazy concept. Looking back years later, I can scarcely believe that I thought I should walk away from a good job with two young children to pursue something that was little more than the fragment of a plan. Other than God's grace, I don't know how I did it. There I was, with no experience in the media industry, believing that I could market a successful radio program essentially on my own. But I felt compelled to do it—and I knew I needed to act in the moment and not delay.

One of the producers came into the recording room where I was working and told me I had received a fax on one of the machines in the office. I told him I would get to it in a moment and wrapped up one of the segments before a commercial break. I took the big silver headphones off, placed them on the table in front of me, and thought about how the show had changed over the course of my time there. It had expanded from a trial test run of one hour per week to three hours. It was exciting and changed constantly as the news did. If a topic was important to people in Indiana, it was important to me and I wanted to talk about it with anyone who called in to share their opinion. Sitting behind a microphone was where I was supposed to be, and I was feeling more and more called to chase the dream of starting my own show. The last of my doubts melted away; I knew it was time to move on.

I walked over to the fax machine and pulled out a piece of paper. It was from Karen at home and read, "Dear Dad, Mom says next Christmas, we need to hang another Christmas stocking by the fireplace. Love, Michael and Charlotte." She was pregnant. My mind raced. I was thrilled, of course, but it was unexpected and seemed like particularly inconvenient timing for our family. I hurried home to join her and celebrate, and I made the choice to trust God and accept that He knew what He was doing.

I have found that oftentimes the paths we are supposed to take in life don't make perfect sense. But God asks us to trust Him when He is calling us out onto the waves of life. That Christmas, I made the leap. I told the Indiana Policy Review board that I was going to leave, and they gave me a generous severance pay of three months to land on my feet.

Of course, the risk didn't impact just me. I wasn't a single guy living on deli sandwiches in an apartment above a garage anymore, as I had been when Karen had met me. I was keenly aware of my wife and children and how my choice would impact the people for whom I needed to provide. But Karen was supportive. She saw that it was a dream of mine, and she trusted that God would lead and guide us in whatever direction we were supposed to go in. Her faith—in God and in me—is the greatest blessing of my life.

My severance funds were helpful, but I knew I would need to find a permanent solution if the idea was going to become a way to provide for my family. I approached a leading radio network in Indiana about joining forces. At the time, it didn't air talk programming, only news and sports. But on the very day that my severance pay ran out, it signed a deal with me. That was an example of what our family calls "God's timing." The station agreed to do a joint venture where it would handle sales and I would market the show to local radio stations. It was incredible. God's faithfulness shone through as I followed where I felt He was calling me. And that crazy idea took shape, a dream of a talk radio show to air across the state.

When Karen gave birth to our third child, Audrey Ann, in August 1994, we had to be on the state-guaranteed fund for medical insurance as a last resort because I didn't have medical insurance with my new job. Audrey entered our lives at a time of deep uncertainty and has often been at the center of times of transition for our family. But when she looked up at me with her big brown eyes for the first time, I felt peace and knew that everything was going to be okay. She has provided that feeling of deep comfort ever since.

At the policy group, I had recognized my dissatisfaction with my life and believed that God would be faithful if I left and pursued the desire He had placed in my heart. I trusted that I could do more—and be more—if I stepped out and trusted Him with my future. When I think back to that time, I can still feel the fear of the unknown that stretched out ahead for our family. But the Bible informs us that we are to trust God with the scary decisions we face in life. It also reminds us that He is there and doesn't leave us. Psalm 118:6 says, "The Lord is with me; I will not be afraid. What can mere mortals do to me?"

There is never a better time than right now to improve your life, to fix your marriage, to do something about anything. There is never a better time to chase your dreams, to trust God with the unknown, and to have faith that He will put the pieces together even when they don't seem to fit.

You're never better than you are right now.

11

Know That Children
Heal Your Heart

Children are a heritage from the Lord.

—PSALM 127:3

My father remains the greatest man I have ever known. Though he was a strict disciplinarian, he had an unmatched love for his children and took a tremendous interest in us. He had high expectations, but they were never without the caring attentiveness of his mentorship. He was a teacher and the coach of our family, and his example, faith, and advice were inspiring to me as I became an adult and started a family of my own.

In the fall of 1983, my first semester at Indiana University School of Law, Indianapolis, turned out to be a stereotypical "paper chase," cutthroat environment. I was in a class with an especially difficult professor who, day in and day out, seemed to single me out. He would call on me without fail, leaving me humiliated when I didn't say the exact right thing. Anytime I answered with "I think," he would thunder, "Mr. Pence, I don't care what you think. I want to know what the court thinks!" I was getting tired of the verbal abuse and was wondering if law school was really for me. In fact, I was considering leaving the school altogether.

After an especially disheartening week, I drove south to Columbus to visit my parents for the weekend. My dad and I walked around the backyard, discussing my first few months of law school.

"He just has it out for me," I explained about the professor. "It's like he's trying to embarrass me."

My dad looked at me with his intense gaze, and all of a sudden, I felt a sting across my cheek as the back of his hand made contact with my face. I was so stunned that I stumbled backward before I saw his hand raising up again for another slap.

I swerved out of the way and instinctively lifted my hand to block him, thrusting his hand up and away from me. His demeanor was still as calm as it had been when we had begun our conversation.

"What are you doing?" I spat, incredulous at that out-of-character moment.

"Why'd you stop me the second time?" he asked, still calm.

"What do you mean? I wasn't going to let you hit me again!" I said.

He leaned forward with the wry smile on his face that always appeared when he was teaching a lesson.

"Maybe that's what the professor is doing, Michael," he said. "You're going to be a lawyer. Somebody's life might be on the line based on whether you can do your job. He might be trying to make sure you can do it when it really counts."

It was a classic Dad moment, and lessons like that would stay with me forever, even after I had to face life without him.

In 1988, the world around me came crashing down when Dad passed away from a heart attack at the young age of fifty-eight.

It devastated our entire family. According to friends who were with him, he collapsed on the sixth hole of the golf course at the Harrison Lake Country Club and was attended to by several of the city's leading doctors. After he died, I asked the doctors who had tended to him about his final moments, and I will never forget what they said. "He was just concerned about you kids and your mom," one of them told me. "He wanted you all to be okay. That's all he cared about."

That was Dad. He was the rock of our household, and I wasn't sure what I would do without him to guide me as I started a family of my own.

I was left in a state of disarray as I grappled with the deepest sorrow I have ever known. His death left a gaping hole in my heart, a void I couldn't fill. I was eager to understand what I needed to do to feel better.

During the 1960s, new psychological discussions about grief began to circulate, primarily stemming from Elisabeth Kübler-Ross's book *On Death and Dying*. The book laid out what came to be known as the five stages of grief: denial, anger, bargaining, depression, and acceptance.[1]

A pastor told me that grief gets better after the first year. Once the "worst firsts"—the first anniversary, first birthday, first Christmas—have passed without a loved one, the grief begins to subside. I looked forward to experiencing that. But although my faith informed me that I shouldn't grieve like those "who have no hope" (1 Thessalonians 4:13), the relief didn't come quickly. I was stuck in every stage all at once. Years went by, and I still felt the pain like a looming, persistent ache in my chest that wouldn't ease. I worried that I was going to feel hollowed out for the rest of my life. I hadn't realized how much love I had been directing toward him, and when he was gone, I felt lost. I had nowhere to put that love.

But in November 1991, the big brown eyes of my newborn son looked up at me in the delivery room of St. Vincent's Hospital in Indianapolis, Indiana. Little Michael Joseph, named after his father and my father, was born.

When Michael was a baby, I used to lie on the couch and place him on my chest while he was asleep. I could feel the comfort—literally and metaphorically—that he brought to me as he slept there. Children are instruments of grace in our lives, and when I felt Michael's breathing slowly match my heartbeat, I felt as though my life was beginning again. My heart began to heal once I had someone else to receive all the love that I had once given to my father.

One night, I had a dream that seemed to capture the emotions of that time. In it, I am napping on the couch without my son, and I wake up to the feeling of tiny fingers tapping my arm. It is Michael, around three years old, standing next to the couch, asking me if he can go outside with Grampa. I look past him to see my dad standing by the door, holding Michael's coat in his hands, waiting. It was exactly what Dad would have done. He would have told Michael to "go ask your father" if he was allowed to go out and play.

The image is as vivid to me as if it had happened in real life: Michael, standing beside the couch, is looking at me with expectant eyes. Dad, patiently waiting, is ready to help Michael get into his coat before heading outdoors. The dream gave me a glimpse of what might have been had my dad not been taken from us. In it, my journey of grief and healing seemed to come full circle.

My dad has been gone for more than thirty years, and not a day goes by that I don't miss him. After he passed away, I was afraid I would stop remembering him, that he wouldn't be as vividly a part of my life as he had been. I didn't need to worry, though; today he is no less a part of my thinking than he was when he was on this earth.

Good fathers never leave you. The only thing that fades is the pain.

It might be counterintuitive to have children after a tragedy has happened; deciding against bringing children into the world might seem like a more rational response. The pain might feel unbearable at times, and I know firsthand how deep it can go. But I've also seen how children can bring healing and renewal. They give us somewhere to direct our love, and by doing so, they mend the wounds of grief. They remind us to delight in the small joys of life, and they teach us to play. They never let us forget the boundless potential of the future, and they give us purpose. If having children isn't an option, surround yourself with little ones when the pit of sorrow seems too deep to escape. For "more are the children" of those "who never bore a child" (Galatians 4:27), which means that the grace of children can be experienced in more ways than having your own.

So if your heart is broken and can't seem to mend, never doubt that children can heal your heart.

12

Let Mom Translate

Her children rise up and call her blessed; her husband also, and he praises her: "Many women have done excellently, but you surpass them all."

—PROVERBS 31:28–29

When my daughter Charlotte was two years old, she began to verbalize many words, usually with limited success. Though I was occasionally able to decipher what she meant, one night I found myself unable to understand her as I got her ready for bed.

Staring up at me with her freshly combed hair pulled back from her face, she was intent on communicating what she needed. She furrowed her brow and tried again and again. "Ma-*shee*-moo-*sha*," she said, enunciating each syllable with focused precision.

Exasperated, I eventually called down the stairs to Karen, who was getting the other two kids into their pajamas for the night. "Karen, she's saying something—I don't know what it is," I said.

"What does it sound like?" she asked.

I told her I had no clue.

She said, "Repeat it to me."

"Ma-shee-moo-sha?" I said, aware of how ridiculous I sounded and sure that she wouldn't be able to understand, either.

"Oh!" she quickly replied. "She wants me to sing the moon song. I'll be right there."

I realized then that I should have admitted earlier that I didn't know what my two-year-old was trying to convey and instead let her mom translate.

I had wanted to understand exactly what my daughter needed, but Karen, being her mother, was better able to provide for her. It was a moment when I was reminded that our kids need both parents, but sometimes in different ways. Thankfully, God gives our spouses the ability to make up for our own shortcomings. You won't always have the right answer for your son or daughter, but your spouse might; and you can help your child by relying on each other.

There may not be a little girl in your home speaking baby talk, but as your children grow, it can sometimes feel as though you and they are speaking different languages. Perhaps they're going through a situation you've never encountered before, or perhaps communication has grown fraught. In such moments, Karen and I would often talk through the issue and decide which of us was best suited to take the lead. Sometimes kids continue to have needs that one parent can meet better than the other. And sometimes all our kids need us to do is listen.

On election night 2012, Michael, Charlotte, and Audrey gave their mom a frame of documents after our victory in the Indiana governor's race was called. Each included pieces of advice she had told them before or during the campaign. Audrey included a phrase Karen had told her when she was going through a difficult transition to a new school. Karen was traveling in Washington at the time, and Audrey was back home in Indiana.

Karen answered the phone when Audrey called and sat down on a park bench, prepared to listen to her daughter's concerns. "I'm listening," she told Audrey. "And I hear you."

Audrey's portion of the gift included these words from Karen, but it also included another sentence that Audrey had written to her: "Greatest words I could ever hear."

Audrey didn't need Karen to try to solve her problems or tell her what to feel; she just needed to be heard by her mom.

In the midst of our busy lives, it's not always easy, but make sure your kids know you are there to listen. Make every effort to understand what they are saying. And when in doubt, let Mom translate.

13

Stop Counting

Give thanks in all circumstances; for this is God's will for you in Christ Jesus.

—1 THESSALONIANS 5:18

O ver the course of my public career, people have often asked me how I'm doing. When I would give an upbeat response, even amid the controversy, criticism, or pressures that are synonymous with American politics, they would express surprise and ask how that could be. I have often responded the same way: "My wife loves me. My kids are healthy. I stop counting after that."

It's true; I stop counting after I take note of the blessings in my life. A friend once told me that when everybody in your family is healthy, you have lots of problems, but when one person isn't healthy, you have only one problem. In other words, when your spouse loves you and your children are in good health, it's easy to get distracted by other problems. If either one of these circumstances changes, everything is put into perspective and nothing else matters.

I try to count my blessings in every scenario, but of course, there have been times when members of my family were having health problems. Those periods made me appreciate the times when we have been blessed by good health and have informed how I respond when that is not the case.

During the fall of 1980, I was sitting in my room at Hanover College when I received a call that my grandmother had taken ill. Mary Cawley was the light of our family—radiant, nurturing, always quick with a smile and boundless encouragement to her grandchildren. When I heard that she was sick, I thought about driving up to see her. But I quickly assured myself that the illness would be short lived and she would be fine. She ended up passing away only a short time later. I'll always wish I had made the drive to visit her one last time.

Only two months later, after struggling with cancer for years, my Grampa Cawley, after whom I was named, fell ill and was admitted to the hospital in Columbus, Indiana. Having missed the opportunity to say goodbye to my grandmother, I did something different that time: I visited him every day.

Arriving one day at the hospital to see him, I was struck by his downcast countenance. His Irish eyes were usually smiling, but this time they met mine in quiet mourning. He was struggling with illness, but it was also clear that he was grieving the loss of his wife, the love of his life. He also knew he was nearing the end of an extraordinary journey that had brought him from the fields of County Sligo in Ireland to the streets of Illinois.

I stood in the hospital room and noticed that it was starkly bare, even though Christmas was just around the corner. Friends and relatives had been sending him cards and gifts, as well as decorations, but they were all piled in a corner. He hadn't hung anything up.

When I pointed out the state of the room, he responded in that Irish brogue I knew so well. "I don't feel a whole lot like celebratin'," he said.

Maybe as proof of my presumptuousness, or perhaps as evidence of the closeness of our relationship, I stood at the end of the bed and told him, "I didn't think Christmas was about us. I thought Christmas was about celebrating the birth of somebody."

He looked at me with his deep-set eyes and didn't say a word. But the next day when I went to his hospital room, it was filled with decorations, including a Christmas tree with lights and cards displayed right where he had told the nurses and orderlies to put them.

Grampa left us and this world on Christmas Eve of that year, and my world grew dimmer without him. Our family was heartbroken. My mother had lost her parents and my siblings and I had lost our grandparents in a short period of time, but we still celebrated Christmas together, just as my grandfather would have wanted.

When the stresses and distractions of your daily life add up and seem to be more than you can handle, it helps to take a step back and remember the rich blessings of the people in your life who really matter. Of course, illness is more than just a distraction, and chronic illness can be a consistent affliction that comes back day after day. Sometimes it doesn't end the way we want it to; sometimes it doesn't end at all until we lose our loved one, which upends our lives and creates a hole that sometimes feels as if it will never be filled. But practicing maintaining a perspective that centers your mind on what really matters in life will help when tragedy comes.

So when your family is in a place of health, take note of it. And even when you face struggles, focus on the blessings in your life.

After that, stop counting.

14

Take Your Daughter to Breakfast

*And he took the children in his arms, placed his hands
on them and blessed them.*

—MARK 10:16

Over Charlotte's sixth birthday, we spent a week at a dude
ranch near Estes Park, Colorado, for a family vacation. We
all stayed in the same small cabin, and I wanted to spend some
time—just the two of us—on her special day. I decided I would
take her out to breakfast.

I called ahead to the lodge to make sure we had a table
and waited outside our cabin for her. She emerged wearing a
denim dress and cowboy boots. When I asked if she was ready
to go, she gave a quick nod. She took my hand, and we walked
together to the restaurant. She would be starting kindergarten that fall, and it felt as though things were really starting to
change. Our middle child would be in school full-time, just like
her older brother, which would be a new season for our family,
but we could tell she was ready. She was excited to go to school,
and her desire to learn was as alive then as it is today.

Over the years, we continued our tradition of having breakfast together on her birthday. It became a time for us to discuss

the year. She spelled out her hopes and dreams during those meals—typically coffee, eggs, and bacon consumed at a local diner. Sometimes she was excited about the future, but often our discussions centered on her fear or confusion about where she was headed. They were times for me to offer advice and counsel—but also, and often most important, to listen.

Throughout my time in Congress, when my children were living at home, I tried to take them with me on work trips that fit their interests. Michael traveled with me to the Kennedy Space Center to watch a shuttle launch, and our family spent one of Audrey's birthdays in Hollywood, California, when she was interested in acting. Although there were times when I failed to do so, I tried to make each one of our kids feel special and give them dedicated time with their dad.

With every year that passed, Charlotte grew from that little girl in cowboy boots to a middle schooler, a teenager, and a young woman. Each breakfast was different from the previous one, because, of course, *she* was different. Every year brought with it new questions, and spending dedicated time with her meant that I could understand her unique challenges. It was helpful to her. But our breakfast tradition meant even more to me.

We didn't have a perfect track record, and there were years we missed our birthday breakfast. But we always did our best to get together on that day or another time near it. The fact that it was an annual tradition meant that we could look back over the year and discuss the victories, the difficult moments, and the big decisions. It gave her undivided attention by her dad, and she would tell you that it made a difference in the person she became.

During her college years, we celebrated her birthday with breakfast at the Illinois Street Food Emporium while I was serving as governor of Indiana. It was a favorite spot of ours, just a few blocks away from the Governor's Residence, and once when we were sitting outside on the patio, I could tell she was lacking confidence and unsure of the future. She didn't know what she was supposed to pursue and was still sorting out who she wanted to be. Sitting across from her at the small iron table at the café, I reminded her of who she was—and the person I knew she could become. I knew she would go on to accomplish all her dreams, and I told her so. More than the specific words I spoke that day, the continuity of our breakfast tradition served as a reminder that her family would always be there, no matter what life brought her way.

In December 2019, our tradition changed forever. We were together, just the two of us, standing in the chapel of the United States Naval Academy in Annapolis, Maryland, and I was getting ready to walk her down the aisle. When I realized that that would be the last time I would be with her while she was still Charlotte Pence, emotions washed over me. I struggled to compose myself as we moved through that historic chapel; my face contorted as I tried to hold back the tears. But as we approached the altar, I looked up and saw the tears on her fiancé's face. When I saw how he was struggling to contain his emotions as he looked at his approaching bride, I felt a peace descend on me. That moment reaffirmed for me that he was the right man for her.

That evening, the wedding reception was held at the Vice President's Residence in Washington, DC. The bride and groom were announced and entered the room to cheering attendees. Karen and I were seated at our table, and she touched my hand to tell me it was time to give the opening toast. Just as my speech at Audrey's wedding would be a few years later, it was a moment heavy with the responsibility of remembering Charlotte's young life up to that point and sending her off to her future.

I have given speeches to tens of thousands of people, on live television, and in front of dignitaries and leaders around the world, but this was different. There were things I knew I needed to say, not only to my daughter on her wedding day, but to her new husband, Henry.

I told Henry that from this day forward, he would be the most important man in her life and that there was a tradition I needed him to keep. I told him it would now be his job to take her to breakfast on her birthday.

That day, I couldn't say the words without my voice breaking with emotion. Now, nearly four years into their marriage, I've been gratified as, year after year, they have kept the tradition alive.

It felt as though a chapter was ending when Charlotte got married, but a new chapter was actually beginning. We are still as close as ever in this new phase of her life, especially as I watch her prioritize spending time with her daughter, the same way I tried to set aside time to spend with my young children.

Our children don't live in our homes very long. Give them what they need most while they are there. Make time for traditions that are just yours and theirs.

Take your daughter to breakfast.

15

Hit the Open Road

The heavens declare the glory of God, and the sky above proclaims his handiwork.

—PSALM 19:1

We live in a digital world, and oftentimes people are content to watch a television show or read about a place on their phones, thinking it is just about the same as visiting a place. I'm here to tell you that it isn't. There is something deeply rich and meaningful in traveling to see a place for yourself: in packing the suitcases, loading up the car, and setting off to see something with your own two eyes.

Early in our family life, we wanted to instill in our children a sense of wonder about the United States. We wanted them to stand among the redwoods, look out over the open ocean, gaze in awe into the Grand Canyon, and marvel at the geysers of Yellowstone. And the best way to see the marvels of our country is by taking a Great American Road Trip.

On those trips, our children learned about our nation's explorations into space at the Kennedy Space Center and surfed off the coast of Malibu. We biked all over Mackinac Island in Michigan, where there are no cars, and indulged ourselves at every fudge shop that caught our eye. We hiked through national parks including Yosemite, showing them what it was like to feel as if they were walking into a painting. We traveled to the islands of Hawaii, where Karen and I renewed our vows on the beach, and we snowmobiled across the otherworldly tundra of Alaska.

As we drove through a national park, I would be inspired by the scene, and from the driver's seat of our minivan, I would often simply say, "Glorious." The beauty of natural landscapes and the splendor of making memories with loved ones deserved the descriptor "glorious" rather than something more generic such as "beautiful." When I asked our kids why I said it was "glorious" instead of beautiful, they would often reply with a groan, "Because it's not just beautiful, Dad. It's because it gives glory to the one who made it." Mission accomplished.

In addition to that enduring lesson, we wanted to show them how to go on adventures, take risks, and try new things. They were able to see the majesty and glory of places all over the country. They met new people, saw how they lived, and found points of common connection. Many of those moments might be lost to memory, but given the chance, I would do it all over again to teach our children how to enjoy this world.

As I grew up, my parents were intentional about going places, too, even if it was just for a drive after church on Sunday. I think it might have been Dad's way of controlling six kids and giving our mom a break. We would drive through the countryside, often in search of the perfect cottage or lake house, one that Mom and Dad said they would buy someday but never did. We didn't need to have a destination; we would just get into the car and go. We saw our community in new ways, taking the back roads and exploring new corners of the place we called home.

When I was in grade school, we went on the quintessential American family road trip, driving all the way across the Midwest to western states and California's Disneyland, staying at Best Western motels along the way. The vacation was memorable, but sadly, we don't have many photographs of it as we lost the film from our camera somewhere along the way. For weeks, the fate of the pictures was a mystery, but when we returned home and developed the one remaining roll of film to watch the footage of our trip, the culprit was evident. There I was on the screen, holding the bag of film at one of the national parks we had visited. The footage captured the very moment I set the bag of film down on a rock and walked away. I'm not sure my family will ever let me live that one down.

When I was governor of Indiana, Karen and I fulfilled one of our lifelong goals and took our children to Israel. I had previously visited the Holy Land with Karen, but showing my children the places where Jesus Christ had lived and walked was a profound experience.

Our family made arrangements to visit Bethlehem, the town where Jesus was born. Our Israeli guide was not allowed to enter with us, which was a sobering reminder of the tensions there. We traveled to the place known as Shepherds' Field, where history and tradition record that "there were shepherds living out in the fields nearby, keeping watch over their flocks at night. . . . Suddenly a great company of the heavenly host appeared with the angel, praising God and saying, 'Glory to God in the highest heaven, and on earth peace to those on whom his favor rests'" (Luke 2:8,13–14). It was Christmastime, and standing under the desert sky in a vast, open field, with the Church of the Nativity visible on another hill just a few miles away, I had the distinct feeling that that night and that Holy Night were not much different. Looking up at the sky, I breathed a prayer of thanks.

We also traveled to the Sea of Galilee, where Jesus first preached, and our kids took a walk at Peter's Bay, where the disciples encountered their risen Savior. As night fell, I'll never forget the moment I came across my son, Michael, standing lakeside, staring into the darkness. I walked up beside him and asked, "You okay?" He said, "This is where it happened, Dad," referring to the story in the book of Matthew where Jesus walked on the water during a storm. In that moment, I could see in his eyes that the words of that story became more real to him. I will cherish that memory for the rest of my life.

Glorious.

The grandeur of the vast stone castles of Yosemite, the dependability of the geysers at Yellowstone, and the hope of Christmas are all moments and places in which God is glorified.

So hit the open road. Find the glory. Experience the natural world, go and see it for yourself, and walk where history happened. Your life will be richer for it.

16

Teach Your Children to Love America

Blessed is the nation whose God is the Lord.

—PSALM 33:12

I love this country. As the son of a small-business man and his first-generation Irish American wife, I had a front-row seat to the American dream. I grew up with the knowledge that in America, anybody can be anybody.

While we were raising our kids, Karen and I made it a priority to share events and places that would encourage them to love this country. From attending community services on Memorial Day to parades on the Fourth of July, we tried to communicate what a privilege it is to be born in America. These events celebrate the values of our country and are a chance for Americans to unite over our shared ideals.

During our years in Congress, we took advantage of living in the nation's capital. On the weekends I stayed in Washington, Karen and I toured the monuments with our kids and visited the Smithsonian Institution whenever we had a chance. As a family, we took long car rides to battlefields on the East Coast such as Antietam, Manassas, and Gettysburg. The open fields became more than plots of land, and the stories of the Civil War and Revolutionary War came to life as we witnessed the ground on which so many men had fought and died for our freedom. With those trips came an appreciation for our armed forces and an understanding that our service members are the reason we are able to live free.

We taught them about our country's military history, and we also included the more recent ideological battles fought and won, especially those of the civil rights movement. Dr. Martin Luther King, Jr., was one of the heroes of my youth. We wanted our kids to know the progress we had made toward a more perfect union in our lifetime, and that history is always in the process of being written.

In 2010, I was approached by the civil rights icon Congressman John Lewis to colead the annual Civil Rights Pilgrimage to mark the forty-fifth anniversary of Bloody Sunday—a day when he, as a twenty-five-year-old aide to Dr. King, had been mercilessly beaten by police in March 1965. His courage and example had helped inspire the passage of the Civil Rights Act of 1968.

I told John that I would be honored to go, but I asked if I could bring my teenagers on the trip. A father himself, he understood my desire to include my family and enthusiastically agreed. Our whole family traveled to Selma, Alabama, for the event.

The night before we made the march from Selma to Montgomery, we had dinner in the basement of Dexter Avenue King Memorial Baptist Church, Dr. Martin Luther King, Jr.'s home church in Montgomery. We spoke with women who had been with Dr. King on Bloody Sunday. Our kids listened with rapt attention as these women told us how they had sung together at the church the night before that fateful day. As history records, hundreds of people marched in peaceful protest across the bridge before they were attacked by members of state law enforcement. On the forty-fifth anniversary of the march, we walked that very route across the Edmund Pettus Bridge alongside Representative Lewis, a hero of the movement. To this day, it is still one of the experiences I am most grateful to have been able to give my children during our time in Congress.

Of course, there were times when our kids didn't want to make the trips and our plans were met with groans and sighs. "Come on, Dad . . . another monument? Another battlefield?" But we were determined. It was our duty as parents to show them the great story of America, even when they weren't excited about it.

It is evident now that each of our children developed a deep and abiding sense of duty to this country, along with, of course, ideas for how it could be improved. All three of them now have families in public service. Michael is a fighter pilot in the Marine Corps, Charlotte's husband is a navy fighter pilot, and Audrey is a Yale Law School graduate who is working as a federal prosecutor.

Inspire your children with a love of America. Tell them stories about what America has meant to you and what it can mean to them. Travel to places that will remind them that freedom is something to be valued and fought for and that the liberties they enjoy today were not free.

17

Follow Your Peace

For God is not a God of disorder but of peace.

—1 CORINTHIANS 14:33

In my life, I have been confronted with many choices, decisions, inflection points, and forks in the road. One thing I've learned is that just because you're struggling with a decision doesn't necessarily mean it's the wrong one; you just need to learn to follow your peace.

I didn't wrestle with deciding to run for Congress in 1988 and 1990. At the time, some people told me to wait a few years and get more experience in politics. There were other positions I could pursue, such as becoming a state Republican Party chairman. Every red light was flashing in my face, but I blew through all of them. I didn't hesitate. I didn't deliberate. Running for Congress was something I wanted to do, so I didn't listen to advice. And, of course, I got crushed. Both of the campaigns we ran in those years collapsed, and I ended up in a place where I was not even sure what I was supposed to be doing with my life anymore.

I didn't just lose the elections; I lost my way.

But in 1999, the opportunity to run for Congress reemerged. I had been approached by the congressman who represented my home district. He was organizing a run for governor and thought I would be a good candidate to take over the congressional seat when he left Congress. Over lunch one day in May, he told me why he thought I should run, but I wasn't sure. It had been my dream forever—but I had let that dream go, hadn't I?

Once again, it was time to make a decision—though this time it was much more difficult than it had been in the past. Everything seemed to be going well, and uprooting our family to pursue something we had already failed twice to achieve seemed like a terrible—and irresponsible—decision.

In the years that had followed the first losses, we had had our son and two daughters and built our dream home, and my radio and television career was starting to gain traction. We had just gotten to a place where we could comfortably pay our bills, and our children were starting school. It felt as though I had taken a leap of faith leaving my job in 1994 when I had trusted God and started my own radio show. How could God be asking me to take a leap of faith again, just a few years later?

Additionally, this time around I knew how terrible it would feel to lose. I had been humiliated not once but twice. Wasn't that enough?

I could almost hear my dad's voice in my head as I lay awake in bed at night thinking about the two paths in front of me. He had been supportive of my run for Congress before he had passed away, and he had even helped me fundraise. But this time around, he would have looked at my steady life and young family and told me that I had responsibilities to consider now. It was not the time to jump out on a ledge and uproot my family. I had a good job. I was building a career in the media. And I had a family that needed me. I had a mortgage to pay. The risk wasn't worth it.

Running for Congress again would mean entering a primary

with several other contenders, selling our dream home, moving back to my hometown in a rental during the election, and dipping into much of our savings—all of that just to potentially lose a third time.

Yes, I would think. *He's right. It's time to grow up.* But whenever I considered staying where I was, in the comfort of my steady income, I would be up all night with fretful sleep. When I pictured jumping into the race, heading toward the unknown, and trusting God, even though I didn't know exactly what the result would be, I slept soundly.

The Bible has many examples of people being called to do something for which they feel unprepared. In fact, God has often chosen people *because* they felt as if they were unfit for the job. It is only by God's grace and through His power that they are able to accomplish what He has planned for them. As the Lord told Paul, "My grace is sufficient for you, for my power is made perfect in weakness" (2 Corinthians 12:9).

One of my favorite examples of this comes from the Old Testament. In it, the angel of the Lord appears to Gideon and says He is sending him to save Israel. But Gideon doubts that he can do it. "'Pardon me, my lord,' Gideon replied, 'but how can I save Israel? My clan is the weakest in Manasseh, and I am the least in my family.'" The Lord's answer was simple: "I will be with you" (Judges 6:15–16).

In response to the gratitude he felt for God's faithfulness, Gideon built an altar, calling it "The Lord Is Peace" (Judges 6:24). God's promise to Gideon was fulfilled, against all odds, and he was able to save his people.[1]

During that time of indecision, I heard a sermon by the same preacher who had made such an impact on me years earlier. Pastor Lake preached about how the Bible tells us that God is a God

of peace and not of discontent. The essence of his message was
that we can feel secure following our peace, knowing that God is
the source of that peace. If we are not at peace about something,
it is typically not from God.

Though indecision is hard, it is often a sign of humility. Indecision, I believe, is part of any good decision. To make a good
decision, you must weigh the benefits and count the costs. And
that was exactly what Karen and I did in 1999.

As a birthday gift, Karen gave me a trip to a Colorado dude
ranch, and we went as a family. The two of us took a horseback
ride together to spend some time alone and talk about what we
should do. It was coming down to the wire, and we needed to
make a decision about the congressional run. This time, not only
was I indecisive, but I wasn't pursuing the seat on my own. My
family's security factored into the decision. But beyond them,
I didn't even really want to do it. I was happy where I was, and
Washington's politics looked more partisan than ever before. I
was about as enthusiastic about the idea of running for Congress
as a cat about being taken to a pool party. I had been there and
tried that. It was done. Couldn't God send someone else?

Karen and I dismounted on the trail and walked to the edge
of the cliff. When we looked out, we saw two red-tailed hawks
flying above us, effortlessly riding the wind currents.

I looked at Karen and said, "Those two hawks are us."

She considered it as we looked out over the span of the
mountains. "If those hawks are us," she said, "then I think we
should run. But if we run, we have to do it like those two hawks
and let God carry us. No flapping."

And so it was decided.

We were going to do it, but we were not going to do it the
same way most people did and the way we had done it before.

We were going to put God first, each other second, and our family third—above our career. We knew what we had done wrong the first few times. This time, we were going to let God lead us. And that meant first saying "yes" to His call.

On the Christmas before that election year, Karen gave me a framed parchment with the words of Jeremiah 29:11: "'For I know the plans I have for you,' declares the Lord, '. . . plans to give you hope and a future.'" We set out on that campaign trusting our peace and the promise of those ancient words. That verse would grace the fireplace of every place we called home during the extraordinary years ahead.

If you have a major decision to make and aren't wrestling over what to do, it's probably the wrong one. But when you seek God's direction on it, He will give you peace. Even when it doesn't make sense, follow your peace.

18

Go Together

Where you go I will go, and where you stay I will stay.
Your people will be my people and your God my God.

—RUTH 1:16

In 1988, during our first run for Congress, Karen attended a reception at the Vice President's Residence in Washington, DC, for candidates' spouses hosted by Second Lady Barbara Bush. At the small reception, Mrs. Bush explained how she was able to have such a strong family while serving in politics. She gave the attendees advice that would have a huge influence on our family more than ten years later.

"Ladies," she said. "You move with your husband."

We never forgot it.

Arriving in Washington more than a decade later, when we finally realized our dream of being elected to Congress, we did just that. It didn't take long to realize that Karen and I were going to stand out by bucking trends, the most obvious example of which was our decision to uproot our family and move to the Nation's capital.

Before 1990, it was much more common for members' families and spouses to move to Washington. We had known Vice

President Dan Quayle and his family after they had left office. They were another strong family who had moved their children to Washington while serving in public life. By the time we arrived in the nation's capital, however, making the move was less popular. We were one of a handful of families who chose to do so, although I understand why most decided against it.

The political scene in Washington is not exactly family friendly. There are lots of late-night votes and early mornings that can get in the way of family life. There were still times that our family didn't get to enjoy dinner together or when I missed a big sports game or performance. When that happened, I sometimes became frustrated with the demanding schedule of a politician, but I remembered that if my family hadn't moved to Washington, those missed moments would be more common.

During those early days of our political career, I sought to be open about how we chose to live. But I never wanted to make people feel bad about the choices they had had to make for their families. During my first term, in an interview with *The Hill*, I discussed the parameters we had put into place to keep our family strong in the midst of a hectic transition to political life. I discussed how we had decided to move our family to Washington, DC. And I explained that Karen and I had tried to establish a "zone"[1] of privacy around our marriage, which turned into the butt of many good-natured jokes after the interview was published.

"I don't want to get in your zone, Pence!" my fellow congressional members would tease, laughing as they gave me a wide berth while passing me in the Capitol building.

I was fine with having a reputation as someone who put my marriage and family first, and I didn't take the teasing personally. They were just having fun, but the article also attracted the attention of people in higher positions of authority in Congress.

One day after voting ended at the Capitol, I stopped into the bathroom and ran straight into Congressman J. C. Watts. At the time, Watts was a big name on campus, and in 1994, he had become the first Black congressman from Oklahoma.[2] He had played college football in the Sooner State. In 1997, he had become the first Black congressman to deliver our party's response to the president's State of the Union address, had been elected Republican Conference chairman the following year, and was widely being discussed as a future presidential candidate.

Feeling like an insecure freshman in that chance encounter with congressional leadership, I politely greeted Watts and stepped aside to leave.

"Pence," he said.

"Yes, sir?" I asked.

"I saw the article in *The Hill*," he said.

I quickly explained to him that I had only wanted to lay out the practices that we were carrying out. I didn't want him to think I was trying to tell anyone else how they should run their families.

He threw his hand towel in the garbage can and looked at me. "My wife and I have already talked about it," he said. "After this term, they're either moving here, or I'm going home."

That surprised me. I knew he had a large family in Oklahoma. His career was starting to take off, and heading in the direction opposite to Washington, DC, was entirely counter to what every political strategist would recommend.

Sure enough, at the end of that term, Watts left Congress and didn't seek reelection. He even spoke publicly about his decision, saying "This business is hard on families. I don't want to do this for the rest of my life. There are other things I want to do and can do. You have to be careful about getting on this treadmill."

He went on to have a vibrant career in the private sector. To this day, he is someone I deeply admire, and that conversation in the bathroom of the US Capitol remained with me throughout my years of public service. A man who seemed to be on top of the world, at the stepping-off point of his career, had backed away from further political opportunities to go home and be with his family. I made a point of remembering his words and never let my own ambitions cause me to forget the values I had brought with me to Washington.

Eventually the conversation surrounding the interview died down. People forgot about the interview until years later, when my practice of not dining alone with a woman other than my wife made headlines. The untold part of that news cycle involved several congressmen who were among the loudest mocking voices in the group. They were men about my age with families and young children. In the years that followed, I would see marriages struggle. I often thought with sadness about how things might have been different for them if they had made choices that weren't as popular with the crowd.

Going against the norm will capture the attention of both well-meaning individuals and others who are not as kindhearted, but it is worth it.

Wherever you go in life, make every effort to keep your family together. They'll be better for it. You'll be better for it.

Go together.

19

Build Levees

Everyone who hears these words of mine and puts them into practice is like a wise man who built his house on the rock.

—MATTHEW 7:24

After leaving office in 2021, we moved home to Indiana. Our new home, nestled into a wooded lot, came with a pond and a farm field to the east.

A small bridge paves the way over the pond, the path creating a natural barricade between our homestead and the rest of the world. The house sits back from the water and consists of stone and brick in a welcoming patchwork. It sits on five acres of land, giving the impression that we are out in the middle of the country. It has enough bedrooms to fit our three children when they come home to visit, and our grandchildren spend long days playing in the pool or shooting hoops. The iron fence around the backyard keeps our dog, Harley, contained as he runs wild at all hours of the day, chasing down squirrels and birds.

To us, it's home.

The house was built fifteen years ago on a solid foundation

of concrete; there was one flaw in its design. Soon after it was completed, the homeowners discovered that the house was positioned on a low area of land that served as a runoff when it rained. When storms came, water poured in from the woods surrounding the house. The owner, realizing his mistake, soon constructed levees all around the house. They kept the rain away by directing it to drains that led to the sump pump and the nearby pond.

Karen and I have witnessed the usefulness of the levees during many a torrential downpour—that is, if everything else is working correctly. One time, the sump pump failed, and we found ourselves with a flooded basement while we were out of town. That needed some fixing, but afterward we understood even more clearly how essential the levees were. They had saved our house time and time again, without our fully appreciating their utility. The mere fact that they existed was the difference between a flood ruining portions of our home and not. And they brought peace of mind, since once they were in place, we didn't have to think about them.

Whenever I look out at the levees, I think of Matthew 7:25, which speaks to building a strong foundation in your life. It says, "The rain came down, the streams rose, and the winds blew and beat against that house; yet it did not fall, because it had its foundation on the rock."

When we got back into politics in 2000 after two defeats, Karen and I did something similar to what the previous owner of our Indiana home had done. We surveyed the situation, and we knew that we needed to act in advance before we were confronted with the distractions of political life. Knowing that the day would come in our public life when the rains would come down, the stream would rise, and the winds would blow, we built levees around our marriage. They took the form of guidelines that we established to protect our marriage and keep it intact. We knew we were heading into the storms of life. And just because our family had been built upon the solid foundation of Jesus Christ, that didn't mean we were necessarily going to make it. We had to put up guardrails to maintain our values and priorities—and to protect our marriage and the vows we had made to each other.

Years ago, I read that our first president had carried a symbol of fidelity to his wife everywhere he went. Since President George Washington was elected at a politically uncertain time, he traveled to many colonies and was often away from home, tending to the needs of the young nation. On his travels, he wore a locket with a picture of Martha Washington inside it. It was a symbol of his love for her, a reminder of his commitment to her, and the last thing he saw every night before he went to bed. I told Karen that story when we were newly married. A few days later, I came home to find a gift from her on my dresser. It was a locket with her picture inside it. To this day, I rarely don't have it on, and I never travel without it.

Displays of loyalty to our spouses matter. A wedding ring is another physical reminder of the vows we make to our spouse when we get married. In front of our friends and family, we tell the world that we are going to be true to that person—and we wear a symbol of that promise on our hand, visible to everyone, for the rest of our lives.

Karen and I had experience making promises to each other before we ever reached the hectic culture of DC. I grew up in the countryside and never saw my dad wear a seat belt a day in his life. Before I got married, I didn't wear one, either, but my wife noticed, and she made me promise that I would start wearing one. Once I saw how serious she was, I promised. It wasn't a casual commitment from me or just something she would have preferred. It was a promise to her, and I knew I had to keep it. For years, every time I got behind the wheel of a car, I buckled my seat belt. In the years to come I found myself in a few accidents, one of them happening when I was governor and we were T-boned, but I came away from all of them unharmed because of the promise I had made—and kept.

Karen and I would make other promises to each other over the years, and some of them became the sources of national conversations. We did so to protect our marriage because we believed that it was the center of our family, and if it was strong, our family would be even stronger than it would have been otherwise.

One rule we made was tossed around the national media years later.[1] When I was vice president, the *Washington Post* published an article with a throwaway line referring to the interview I had done with *The Hill* a decade and a half earlier.[2,3] In that interview, I had told the reporter that I had promised my wife that I wouldn't dine alone with a woman other than her. That was widely ridiculed in 2017 as sexist and something that prevented women from rising to positions of power in my office. Nothing could be further from the truth. I've served alongside many talented women during my years in office and employed many more. My first lieutenant governor was a woman, and women have served in senior roles on my congressional staff and in my governor's cabinet with great distinction. To suggest that women needed to have a dinner alone with me to excel in their careers is, frankly, demeaning and insulting to them.

Having that rule in place protected my colleagues as well. What if being invited to a private meal together made a woman in the office uncomfortable, but she felt that she couldn't decline? And how much more at ease would young people in politics be speaking to both Karen and me at an after-work party, rather than just me? Being aware of the dynamics of office hierarchy and culture isn't exclusionary, it's common sense.

There are many people who do things they regret because they haven't planned in advance. My faith teaches me that God's grace and forgiveness extend to these individuals, too, and I've watched as marriages have been healed even after the heartache of infidelity and separation. But it's worthwhile to make a plan *before* you are in a situation where you could violate your marriage vows. Don't assume that it won't happen to you. The stakes are too high not to have clear guidelines for your own behavior.

Building levees might serve to keep negative influences out of your family life, but it will likely keep desirable opportunities out, too. You might be excluded. You might be laughed at, and people might avoid you because they perceive you to have values that don't make sense to them. It may seem as if it would be easier to achieve your goals if you were more flexible.

Following the patterns of our society might be more convenient, but storms are always on the horizon. Jesus said that "everyone who hears these words of mine and puts them into practice is like a wise man who built his house on the rock. . . . But everyone who hears these words of mine and does not put them into practice is like a foolish man who built his house on sand. The rain came down, the streams rose, and the winds blew and beat against that house, and it fell with a great crash" (Matthew 7:24, 26–27).

It's hard to build your family, career, and marriage on principles that honor Christ and are in accordance with His teachings.

Even when you put Him at the center of it all, the distractions of the world can come in and flood the very fabric of your life. By building levees, by making decisions to put your marriage first, you can protect your treasures.

Don't ever doubt that the wind and the rain will come, so build your levees and, I promise you, by God's grace your house will not fall.

20

Find the Lizard

*You have heard that it was said to the people long ago,
"Do not break your oath, but fulfill to the Lord the vows
you have made."*

—MATTHEW 5:33

K aren and I first ran for Congress in 1988, long before we had children, but it would be ten years later before we would run—and win—a seat in the US House of Representatives. So when we ran in 2000, it was the first time we did so as a family. Michael, a third grader at the time, was especially invested in the election. He had a youthful enthusiasm for the political process, but he knew that if we won, it meant that we would move to Washington, DC, away from all his friends.

While I was focusing my attention on the campaign, Karen was focused on ensuring that the kids were okay and looking for ways to set their minds at ease. Along the way, she promised Michael that whether or not we won the election, we would get him a present when it was over. He knew exactly what he wanted: a small lizard, specifically, a bearded dragon.

After lots of fundraisers, fairs, and parades, we were successful. Much of our success could be attributed to our kids, as Michael and his sisters traveled countless country miles to earn us the right to represent Indiana in our nation's capital. We began preparations to move east and, true to her word, Karen told Michael that we would buy him a lizard as soon as we arrived in Washington. I thought we would eventually get the lizard, maybe after we were settled in the house we were renting, but Karen, as usual, had a different idea. She intended to keep her word on day one.

The day after we made the ten-hour drive to Washington in our minivan with our dog, cat, and three kids, Karen began the search for a bearded dragon. That was before Google Maps, instant lists of stores, and products at our fingertips. She searched the phone book for pet stores across northern Virginia and headed out. As afternoon turned to evening, she had visited more than half a dozen stores to find the type of lizard Michael wanted. She wouldn't come home without it. I started to worry about her, but just before the kids' bedtime, she arrived home carrying a pet store box. Our boy was grinning ear to ear. Michael had his bearded dragon, as promised. The reptile had rough tan scales covering his body and a soft, squishy neck that puffed up and turned into a pointy beard when he was threatened. Michael named him "Gollum" after a character in *The Lord of the Rings*, a book series I had read to him. Oddly enough, we ended up calling the lizard "Bob" more often than we called him his given name.

I don't have a particular affinity for scaly creatures, and I thought it was a disgusting pet. But Michael loved it, and perhaps surprisingly, his mother came to love that little lizard, too. Karen would place him on a towel in the living room to keep him near her while she vacuumed and cleaned the house. Bearded dragons are known for being affectionate with people and liking to spend time with their owners.[1] He was a fun addition to our household. More important, he was a reminder of the promise we had made to Michael—and evidence that we had kept it.

I learned a timeless lesson from my wife that day: when your family is coming up on big changes, give them something to look forward to. No matter what happens, they will have a positive outcome to associate with the new patterns being introduced into their lives. Karen was an exemplar in keeping our promises to our kids, and her devotion to them has been an inspiration to me.

Making promises is easy, but keeping them is hard. Though I tried to do so, I didn't always follow through on my promises, and there were times when I disappointed my family. For example, I promised to read a book series to each of my children. I succeeded in reading *The Lord of the Rings* to Michael and several of C. S. Lewis's Narnia books to Charlotte. But although I started a book with Audrey, I never finished it. Over the years, she reminded me, but life seemed to become busier and busier, and I thought I didn't have time. I let her down. I didn't keep my promise, and I regret it to this day.

Promises are not always going to be the same, depending on the person you're making them to. What your family needs and what will make them most excited during a time of transition will be different for everyone. Choose something together—or better yet, let them pick—so there will be a prize waiting on the other side of a big change regardless of what happens. The content of the promise doesn't matter, but making—and keeping—the promise does.

The Bible tells us in 2 Peter, "The Lord is not slow to fulfill His promise" (2 Peter 3:9). Similarly, as parents we should not be slow to fulfill the promises that we've made to our children. I saw firsthand the power of a promptly kept promise. So did our son. And I believe that in that moment he got a glimpse of the way God keeps His promises to us.

Making promises establishes a foundation of trust on which your family will rely during transitions. It also carries a weight that should not be taken lightly. If you fail to follow through on a promise, be sure to admit it and apologize, and let your regret motivate you to do better in the future.

Make promises to your family, then work to keep them.

Find the lizard.

21

Teach Your Kids to Speak Their Dreams

Take delight in the Lord, and he will give you the desires of your heart.

—PSALM 37:4

I sometimes encounter young people who are shy as they approach me for a picture. Their parents, standing alongside them, let me know that their child is the class president at school or is interested in politics. When I ask these young people what they want to do with their lives, they shuffle their feet and reply, "I want to be a . . ."

With that, I always say, "You just passed the first test."

When they ask what I mean, I explain, "You just told me what you want to be. That's the first step: you've got to speak your dreams."

Saying our dreams out loud can be nerve-wracking, but it is the first step to going where we want to go. People are often afraid to admit what they want to do for fear of failure or embarrassment, but spoken dreams hold us accountable and drive our actions. As parents, we have a unique opportunity to foster this courageous pursuit in our own children. Whenever they display an interest in a particular topic or share a hope for their future, we should encourage them.

I can still see Michael in his airplane Halloween costume when he was five years old. The cardboard wings dragged on the ground as he walked from house to house in our neighborhood on the south side of Indianapolis, entirely comfortable in the outfit. It fit him, or at least it fit his dreams. As a little boy, he loved planes. He also showed an interest in the military, never leaving the house without his plastic army men.

His fascination with flight continued into his young adult years. In high school, we encouraged him to take flight classes at the school's career center, and he got his pilot's license before he graduated. At Purdue University, he majored in physics before recognizing that he needed to follow his true passion and switching his degree to flight. After college, he entered the Marine Corps's Officer Candidates School and was selected for aviation.

There are few times in my life when I have been filled with more pride than I was at his commissioning ceremony. I watched as he stood stock still alongside his fellow marines. When it was his turn, he walked to the front, placed his hand on a Bible, and took the same oath I have taken in my public life. He answered the call to serve and defend his country at home and abroad. It's been a privilege to watch as he and his family make sacrifices to do that. Today, he is a captain in the Marine Corps and an F-35 fighter pilot, and every time I think of him taking off in that stealthy fighter jet, I see that little boy once again.

Our daughter Charlotte was a voracious storyteller and as a young child could often be found sitting cross-legged in the backyard telling tales to her assembled stuffed animals. Many nights, we would hear her talking to her little sister, Audrey, in the bedroom they shared. She concocted complex stories to help her sister fall asleep. Even when she didn't yet know how to write, she drew squiggly lines in her journal as if they were words, itching to get something down on the page. We moved one of our old Macintosh computers to her room when she was in middle school so she could have her own computer to compose the stories she imagined. In college, she double majored in digital cinema, with a focus on screenwriting, and English. Later, she worked in the film industry and got her master of theological studies degree with a focus on religion, literature, and culture at Harvard Divinity School.

When she was growing up, I often told her, "You're my writer," and I would tease that she was going to write a book about me one day. She would invariably roll her eyes, but of course, she did.

I still have a copy of the little book she made called "A Congressman Through a Twelve-Year-Old's Eyes." As an adult, she brought the stories of our family to the wider market and published *Where You Go: Life Lessons from My Father*. She also wrote three children's books that Karen illustrated, one of which became a bestseller, and works as a journalist. She even helped to get this book onto the page.

Our younger daughter, Audrey, always had a heart for justice. Throughout her young life, she performed on the stage and participated in model United Nations. Schoolwork and studies were always a natural gift for her. In college, she wasn't sure what career she wanted to pursue, but she studied international relations and spent time abroad in the Balkans, Turkey, the Middle East, and Africa.

After some deliberation toward the end of college, she decided to take the LSAT and pursue law school. I always tell young people who are considering a similar path that they will enjoy law school if they enjoy studying for the LSAT. It's a good litmus test. That was true for Audrey, and she excelled on the exam and did exceptionally well at Yale Law School. During her time at Yale, she did pro bono work helping individuals applying for restraining orders, and she is now working as a federal prosecutor.

Once our children speak their dreams, our job is to believe in them. As parents, it's tempting to want to push our kids into one direction or another. We often think we know what's best. We want to give them a solid start in life and perhaps help them avoid the pitfalls we encountered. But learning to speak their dreams, without self-consciousness or insecurity, is how they uncover the gifts they have and how they are meant to use them.

Parents have another role, too. We have a special responsibility to lead by example. We show our children how to speak their dreams by speaking our own.

It's natural for young people—and adults—to avoid being honest about their dreams. Somewhere along the way, they might have been told that their goals were unattainable or it was unlikely that they would ever accomplish them. Reversing this message is a lifelong effort. The best way for parents to show their children how to tune out the discouraging voices of the world is to run after their own dreams.

For example, Karen's lifelong dream was to be a schoolteacher, which she would achieve for thirty years in public and Christian elementary schools. She is also an accomplished watercolor artist who took her talents to art shows across

Indiana and was commissioned to paint hundreds of home watercolors, and as second lady, she even painted a watercolor of the Vice President's Residence. Our children saw her live her dreams in the classroom and on the canvas.

After each campaign, Karen and I would give a small gift to each of our children on election night to thank them for their work. For us, campaigning was always a family affair. From the time our kids were just starting school, we made it clear that they were always welcome to come to any campaign event, but our policy was that they didn't *have* to attend anything. If they wanted to be involved in politics, they could be, but there were no expectations or requirements.

On election night 2012, after I was elected governor of Indiana, our family huddled together. We wanted some privacy to pray and quickly exchange gifts before we headed to the stage that had been set up for my acceptance speech. The only place we could be alone was in a bathroom in the suite where we had been watching the results, so we shut the door and stood in a circle as Karen and I presented our gifts to the kids.

The kids surprised Karen by pulling out a gift bag in return. She started to tear up as she pulled out three interconnected silver frames. The individual sections each held a notecard. One of them read, "You teach your kids how to fight for their dreams by fighting for yours."

Our children are watching us. They find the confidence to engage with their passions by seeing us do the same.

So speak your dreams to your children. Through your example, they will learn to speak and live their own.

22

Let Music Minister to You

Make music to the Lord with the harp.

—PSALM 98:5

*E*ncourage* means "to inspire with courage."[1] Throughout my life, a dependable source of encouragement has been music. God uses music to uplift and enliven us and to remind us of His promises. Whereas reading God's Word brings understanding, comfort, and instruction, when the words of those passages are put to music, they provide an entirely new source of strength. This may be in part because of the importance of worshiping the Lord. Of course, you can worship without music, but I have found that singing prayers and praises to God creates a unique connection. It adds emotional dimension and has the ability to influence us in renewed ways. Personally, it has given me hope and fortitude when I felt lost, confused, and weary.

I am indebted to the ministry of several musical artists. Their music impacted the decisions I made in my career and ultimately encouraged me to keep my perspective on Christ, even when times were difficult. I'd like to share a few songs that have meant something to me and show how they influenced my life.

Even after I came to faith in college, I felt a weight on my shoulders of how much I wanted to do in life. From very early on, I was fascinated with public service. God placed that desire in my heart from a young age, and I was confident that my calling was to serve in public life someday. But as a young person about to enter the workforce, I struggled to figure out what role I was going to play. I was struggling with the pressure of knowing that I wanted to do great things in my life and be of influence but not understanding how—or if—I ever would. At the time, I heard the song "All I Ever Have to Be" by Amy Grant. It says that "When the weight of all my dreams/Is resting heavy on my head,"[2] God reminds us that He created us and all we need to be is what He made us to be. That stopped me in my tracks when I first heard it. The song made me realize that I didn't have to be great or unique; I just had to be what God created me to be, and He would handle the rest. I was enough just as He had made me. I didn't need to try to be anything more.

Casting Crowns is another band whose songs have had a profound effect on me. Their song "Voice of Truth"[3] has resurfaced in various seasons of my life and reminded me to trust God's Word. The song describes what it feels like to take chances in life: it feels impossible, but when the world is stacked against us, there is a Voice that is ready with encouragement. Our fears shrink and our adversaries don't seem so strong when we seek Him and His help.

I used to put the cassette of that track into my Walkman and listen to it repeatedly. When I was trying to decide if the time was right to step out of my comfort zone and run for office, the lyrics of the song gave me perspective. Instead of succumbing to the fear of other people's opinions, the possibility of failure, and the shame of humiliation, the song reminded me to listen to Him. When the voices of the world tell me that I'm going to fail, that I'm going to crash, that I'm going to find myself embarrassed and isolated, I listen to the Voice of Truth instead.

During my time as vice president, I invited Casting Crowns to the White House when they were in town for a concert. I told them that one of the reasons I was there at all was because of the encouragement I'd received from "Voice of Truth." The members of the band were glad to hear that and polite as I recounted to them how much the song meant to me, but I felt compelled to press the point. When I asked which of them had written it, they pointed to one of the members, Mark Hall. I asked if I could give him a hug, right there in the West Wing, to thank him for what the song had done for me. His song changed who I had become for the better. It was deeply moving for me to be able to thank him in person.

On their last night in town, I attended the band's concert. Toward the end, they announced that they were going to sing an extra song that wasn't part of the program. They told the crowd it would be instrumental, and they were dedicating it to someone who had told them how much it had meant to him.

It was "Voice of Truth."

———

On my drives into work during my years serving in Congress, I listened to the songs of Michael W. Smith as I made my way to the Hill. Almost every time my silver Chevy Malibu reached the Theodore Roosevelt Bridge, where Interstate 66 carried me from northern Virginia into the District of Columbia, the sixth song on his 2001 album *Worship*, "Above All," would begin to play. The song grounded me and settled my heart, reminding me that God is "Above all powers / Above all kings."[4] The vanities of our nation's capital have the capacity to distract us from our core convictions. Working every day in the US Capitol, with access to the entire country via the members of the press, can easily make you think you are the most important person in every room. I knew I was doing important work for my constituents, but I had to remember that God was using me, that whatever our team was able to accomplish was because of His blessings and grace; it wasn't because of anything I had done on my own.

Several decades later, on March 28, 2023, I would make my way to Liberty University for the consecration of the School of Law. At the outset of the service, Michael W. Smith, with whom I had become friendly during my time as vice president, sat at a small keyboard and led a worship service. I turned to the president of the college and joked that we were letting Smith off easy since we were singing along with him. The president laughed and asked if I had a favorite song of his, to which I replied that I did.

"You should ask him to sing it," he said.

After the worship portion of the ceremony ended, I approached the podium to deliver my speech. I told the crowd of students, faculty, and guests that I was honored to be there and acknowledged the distinguished attendees. Then I veered away from my prepared remarks and told the story about my drives into Capitol Hill as a young congressman and how the song "Above All" had become a daily encouragement to me. I turned to Smith and asked him to play the song, adding that the president of the college had given me permission to do so. To my great delight, he obliged.

As he returned to the keyboard and quietly sang "Above All," my mind drifted back to those early days of my political career, and his music ministered to me one more time.

After twelve years in Congress, I returned home to Indiana after being elected the fiftieth governor of the Hoosier State. After two successful years of passing historic tax relief and education reform, I was faced with a challenging time as governor. In the spring of 2015, Indiana enacted the Religious Freedom Restoration Act and my state came under attack as Hoosiers were mischaracterized as intolerant. I felt the need to respond in a way that would help people on both sides of the issue come together and feel heard. Perhaps predictably, people on the political left argued that I hadn't done enough. But many conservatives also criticized me. When your opponents come after you, you expect it. But when friends start to publicly criticize what you've done, knowing that you did your best to lead in a manner worthy of the people you represent, it's more difficult. Just a few months earlier, commentators had labeled me a potential 2016 presidential candidate, but that faded away after the controversy.

Soon after the news about the law had died down, I heard a song during a family vacation on an album by Steven Curtis Chapman entitled "Glorious Unfolding." The words "I know this is not / Anything like you thought / The story of your life was gonna be"[5] came through my headphones. It felt as if the message was meant just for me. I had thought that my life in politics was over, but the song reminded me that God had more in store for my life than I ever could have planned. As I would soon find out, God did have more for my story after all, just like the song says.

Learning how to rely on and listen to Him during that time prepared me for what was to come. A little over a year later, I was being considered as a vice presidential candidate by a brash, loud, opinionated New Yorker who won the Republican presidential nomination. Once again, I would need to listen to the Voice of Truth.

I received calls from well-meaning friends who told me it would be a mistake to be on Donald Trump's ticket. I heard from colleagues who said that it would be the end of my career, and some Christians even told me that I couldn't possibly run with someone who had lived so different a life from mine. But I had peace about whatever was going to happen. I knew that we weren't pursuing the position. We were letting God carry us to that place if He wanted us to serve there. We made ourselves available, but we never tried to audition for the role. If that was where God was calling us, we would listen to Him and faithfully go. And if He wasn't calling us there, we would have peace in that, too, because we trusted Him.

When you are in a position of leadership, whatever it is, difficult situations will arise, and many people will have opinions on how you handled them. But when the laughter and discontent seem to be too loud to hear anything else, music will remind you to Whose voice you should be listening. Let music minister to you.

23

Beat Yourself

Do you not know that in a race all the runners run, but
only one receives the prize? So run that you may obtain it.

—1 CORINTHIANS 9:24

During middle and high school, my brothers and I were involved in various athletic and extracurricular pursuits. I was active on the speech and debate team, as well as the wrestling team, while my brothers were involved in sports such as football and swimming.

My dad had a surprising rule regarding those activities: he didn't attend our games and meets. On the surface, this doesn't seem very supportive. However, his reasoning revealed quite the opposite. He didn't attend the events because he wanted his sons to do their best, but not for him. He didn't want us to go out there and try to win so he would be proud of us. He saw how many children tried to prove themselves in those situations and ended up miserable, their happiness dependent on whether they got a nod of approval from their father. Instead, he wanted us to be proud of ourselves, no matter how we performed.

Despite being absent from those events, he had a bit of advice. He used to tell us that the only person we needed to beat was ourselves. It didn't matter if we did better than our competitors. The only real measurement of success was whether we had taken to the field, the podium, the pool, and left knowing that our performance, drive, and effort that day had been better than they had been when we tried in the past.

I think that might have been one of the reasons why my dad loved to play golf. Every time he teed off, he was looking to do better than others on the course, but he was primarily trying to beat his own best score. Golf is a game against yourself, which makes it uniquely challenging.

———

During our two failed congressional runs early in our married life, Karen and I didn't just lose the elections; we lost our way. I didn't live up to the standard of faith that I had for myself. When all was said and done, I had to face the fact that I had become someone I didn't want to be. I had engaged in negative campaigning, which had included running television ads that went after my opponents in an unfair and—frankly—mean way. I had been more interested in talking about what I was against rather than what I was for. I had been full of myself and promoted my own abilities instead of my party's ideals.

Karen and I also hadn't prioritized our marriage and family time as well as we could have. We had campaigned relentlessly, but she was working full-time as a second-grade teacher, so a lot of the election season had involved my traveling by myself. When we could go to an event together, she would often get home from a long day of teaching and we would drive to the next Republican dinner on the schedule. It was less obvious before we had children, but looking back, I'm sure that we didn't put our family ahead of the campaign. Not only did we get caught up in a campaign that didn't square with our values, but we invariably did not put each other first.

So when the opportunity came for us to run again ten years later, I ran not to win but to honor God, to run a campaign we would be proud of and treat others the way we wanted to be treated. Those were my goals. In my mind, I wasn't running against the other candidates in the primary or even against the Democratic candidate once the general election began. My opponent in 2000 was Mike Pence in 1990. I saw the election as an opportunity to prove to people that I had become a different person. I wanted to run against the arrogant, negative guy who had taken to the field unsuccessfully in 1988 and 1990. I wanted to beat him.

In essence, my dad's principle was the foundation of that third congressional run. That meant that the outcome didn't matter as much as the way I ran the race. The result was in God's hands. If we won, we won. If we didn't, I still wanted to be proud of the person I had been during the campaign.

That was a different way of measuring my success. Win or lose, who was I going to be on the other side? Campaigning in a way that made me happy with the answer was my goal, but it was going to take work. I would have to be honest about the errors and shortcomings I had struggled with in the past—and the ways in which I still fell short. Then I would have to do it better. Just as my dad had taught me years earlier, I was going to do my best to beat myself.

That meant that I would need to avoid making personal attacks against my opponents, which is a difficult thing to do in the world of politics. I would need to run ads that would lay out the bad policies my opponents propagated, while also painting a picture for a brighter future. I would have to take a hard look at my errors in the previous campaigns and make a 180-degree turn, even if it meant I wasn't successful in the end. I would have to take the unpopular political path—the one of kindness and goodwill toward people with whom I disagreed.

In the end, we won that election, but more than that, by God's grace, we won back the self-respect that comes when we are aligned with our highest standards.

My son, Michael, once said, "My dad is a very competitive person." He's right. And I believe that competition is a good thing. It's healthy and should be welcomed because it spurs us out of complacency and toward self-improvement. It helps us achieve more than we would had we not been pushed by the pursuits of others. But the best type of competition is the ongoing one we have with ourselves. When you work toward beating yourself instead of doing better than the people around you, peace and assurance come with doing so. When you measure yourself against yourself and see improvement, you're a winner.

The victory of accomplishing this is more fulfilling than winning against other people will ever be. In the competitions of life, play against the person you used to be. And beat yourself.

24

Take Time to Pay Your Respects

If you owe . . . respect, then respect; if honor, then honor.

—ROMANS 13:7

Though Abraham Lincoln was born in Kentucky and entered politics from Illinois, Hoosiers take great pride in the fact that our sixteenth[1] president grew up in Indiana. Referring to our home state, Lincoln wrote, "There I grew up."[2] Today, Lincoln's boyhood home is a memorial site in Spencer County, Indiana.[3] The county maintains several locations that honor and remember President Lincoln's early life in Indiana, where he lived for fourteen of his formative years as a child and young adult.[4]

When I was governor of Indiana, I traveled to the southern corner of the state for an event at the president's boyhood home. At the conclusion of the event, I was determined to visit a location on the grounds that is often overlooked: the final resting place of the president's mother, Nancy Lincoln.

Nancy Hanks Lincoln was born in Virginia in 1784.[5] She had three children, and even though she died when Abraham was only nine years old, she had a large influence on the future president's life. She encouraged his education and was a key reason that he placed such a high value on kindness and honesty.[6] She was deeply rooted in her faith and read her Bible more often than she read the newspaper. Lincoln is reportedly believed to have told William Herndon, his biographer and legal partner, "All that I am or ever hope to be I owe to my angel mother."[7]

Before departing the memorial in Indiana, I informed my staff that I was going to walk to Pioneer Cemetery. I took a stroll through the wooded area and found a metal fence surrounding the small grave site. There were a few other gravestones nearby, underneath the tall oak trees whose leaves provided a generous shade. The sun peeked through the layer of leaves above and cast pockets of light onto the grass surrounding the memorials. I walked up to the pointed gravestone I was looking for and saw a name: Nancy Hanks Lincoln. I smiled as I took note of something I had never thought of before in all my studies of Lincoln. It turns out that Abraham Lincoln and I have at least one thing in common: both of our mother's names are Nancy. I think that's probably the extent of it, but it was a nice connection nonetheless.

While a few staff and park rangers looked on, I bowed my head and said a silent prayer of thanks for a woman who had shaped a boy who would save the union. The life that she modeled for her son had improved not only his own life but the course of our history as a nation. My gratitude to her in that moment was profound. As we prepared to leave, a park ranger thanked me for visiting Mrs. Lincoln's grave site and informed me that the last political figure to do so had been the late senator Robert F. Kennedy during a similar visit to the memorial in 1968.[8] Our modern culture seems to pay little heed to the tradition, but I make a practice of paying my respects at the final resting place of our nation's leaders whenever I visit a memorial.

Not everyone has the opportunity to visit historical sites,

but we can pay tribute to people from the past by doing so within our own families. Whenever you have the opportunity, visit the grave sites of your ancestors. It will make them more real to you and enliven the stories you grew up hearing. Several years ago, my daughter Charlotte went by the cemetery in southern Indiana where my dad had been laid to rest. She had never met her Papa Pence, but as she was visiting home one day, she wanted to pay her respects. She realized she had nothing to leave at the grave site, having not brought any flowers, but she found a few loose golf balls in the back of my car and placed them in the flower holder. A few weeks later, my mom mentioned that she had seen the golf balls, which held a special significance since Dad had loved the sport. When Charlotte said she was the one who had left them, I told her she had no idea just how perfect that gift was.

Americans used to have more respect for our nation's history, for the people who sacrificed to make this country the beacon of freedom that it is today. I've watched in recent years as some people attempt to erase parts of our past, trying to cancel the memory of what has gone before. Forgetting the past is wrong and misguided. As the saying goes, those who forget history are destined to repeat it. We can acknowledge the injustices of the past and still be grateful to the people who brought forth the nation.

The staff working at these locations are often surprised to hear that I'd like to visit the final resting places of our nation's heroes. In a sense, this is understandable: being around a graveyard may make some people uncomfortable. Others may wonder, *What difference does it make to pay your respects if the people you want to acknowledge are already dead?* But I believe it's important to pay tribute to those who have gone before, to honor all they meant to America. The Bible says, "If you owe . . . respect, then respect; if honor, then honor" (Romans 13:7). Part of our duty is to respect those who have come before us. And by seeing their final resting places, we bring them out of the history books and family legends and into our lives.

In my first year as vice president, I did the same when visiting friends in Vermont. After flying Air Force Two into Burlington International Airport, we boarded a multicar motorcade and began the drive in a rural area of the state. The leaves were changing, and their vibrant colors seemed to light up the landscape with a sunsetlike glow. Our host had mentioned to me that our drive would take us near Plymouth Notch, the hometown of President Calvin Coolidge, and he arranged a tour of the site. When we arrived at the historic district, we went by the Visitor Center in the two-street town.[9] A helpful guide showed us the general store that Coolidge's father had run and where the former president had also worked. We also visited the Coolidge home and stood in the small sitting room where Coolidge had taken the oath of office[10] following the death of President Warren G. Harding in 1923. I found myself in awe, standing in the room where he had been sworn in as president. I thought about his humble beginnings and the humility with which he had led our nation. To most people Coolidge is not a particularly memorable president, but he helped improve the economic status of our country and was a steady hand at the tiller during the Roaring Twenties. As we were leaving town, I asked the staff at the Coolidge memorial where the president had been laid to rest. They pointed me in the direction of Plymouth Notch Cemetery, a few miles down the road. So, of course, we went.

I'll never forget pulling up to the humble cemetery as the Secret Service pulled the massive black SUVs over to the side of the small country road. We must have been quite a spectacle. I got out of the car and walked up a few steps to a modest row of headstones with the names of Coolidge family members on them. One stone stood among them, not much different from or even larger than the others beside it. On it was written "Calvin Coolidge" with the dates of his life: July 4, 1872 to January 5, 1933. The only defining feature of the gravestone was the presidential seal engraved into the top. Modest to the last, the president's gravestone appeared one among many generations of his family—no more, no less, save the seal of the highest office of the land.

I marveled at the sight and was pleased to find tangible evidence of the humility by which the man and president lived his life. Though other presidents have grand final resting places, which is their right, Coolidge is simply laid to rest in a family plot in a cemetery in his hometown.

My family had similar experiences at Montpelier, the Virginia home of James Madison, and at the Ronald Reagan Presidential Library & Museum in Simi Valley, California.[11] I especially wanted my children to understand President Reagan's legacy, as his political service had inspired my career in the Republican Party. When President Reagan had passed away, Karen had taken our children downtown to stand along the route where the riderless horse would bring the caisson bearing his casket. The moment felt full circle, as one of my earliest memories was hearing the *clip-clop* of the hooves of the horses carrying the remains of President John F. Kennedy.

As vice president, I was grateful to attend a church service in Memphis on the holiday weekend commemorating the life of Dr. Martin Luther King, Jr. I toured the museum that had been built around the motel where he was assassinated. I walked the grounds, and I looked into the room leading out to the balcony where the life of the civil rights hero had been taken.

I did the same when visiting Dallas, Texas, and traveled to Dealey Plaza to see where another hero of my youth, President John F. Kennedy, had been assassinated. And during my first year in Congress, I took my son, Michael, to Arlington National Cemetery, where we walked among the somber white crosses marking the final resting places of American heroes of every war our country has fought since the Civil War. Before the day was out, we walked to the grave site of President John F. Kennedy to pay our respects. I caught a glimpse of the eternal flame flickering above the late president's grave, and I turned around and gazed across the Potomac River at the Lincoln Memorial and the Capitol, almost in shadow as the sun went down. I realized that I was standing at the grave site of a president who had inspired me when I was roughly as old as my son. As a kid, I had heard how Kennedy had served in Congress and gone on to be a senator and then the president. Learning of his career had made me realize that someday, maybe, I could be a congressman from my hometown, too. I breathed a prayer of thanksgiving for the privilege God had given me to have lived out my boyhood dream.

Visiting the final resting places of historical figures and our ancestors is right and honorable. But it also makes these remarkable Americans more real to us. Today, it seems that people are more interested in tearing down monuments rather than honoring people from the past and using their example to find answers for our future. When I consider the state of our nation, I can't help but think that the future of our country will be improved if Americans take the time to think of these historical figures as more than just facts to memorize, to understand who they were, what they struggled with, and how they came to build the incredible country we live in today.

We owe a debt to those who have gone before, who gave so much so we could enjoy the blessings of our lives. Visiting the grave sites of historical figures and our relatives connects us to them in ways the bare knowledge of American history—and our own personal histories—simply can't. Take time to pay your respects.

25

Go First

Parents are the pride of their children.

—PROVERBS 17:6

When Charlotte was a little girl, we took a family vacation to Florida, which is still one of our favorite places to relax on the beach. During our trip, she had an experience that was painful at the time yet would later serve as a lesson in how to face her fears.

She and her siblings were playing in the sand and suddenly spotted dolphins close to the shore. Michael, always rushing in headfirst without a helmet, took off running, plunging into the water to try to catch up to them, and Charlotte was close on his heels. A few moments later, she was running back out of the water, screaming and crying, with her foot covered in blood.

I scooped her into my arms and ran her up to the hotel room where we were staying. We called our pediatrician, who told us she had likely been stung by a stingray, which we quickly found to be true based on the indentation the stinger had left on her heel. The doctor told us to soak her foot in hot water to neutralize the toxin, so I joined her by submerging my own foot in the nearly scalding bathwater. We took her to the emergency room to make sure the stinger wasn't stuck in her foot and found more stingray victims there, seated in wheelchairs with buckets of hot water for their wounds.

A few years passed, and Charlotte was still afraid of stingrays. Karen wanted to help her overcome her fear and took her on a trip to the local aquarium. Karen had heard of a tank of stingrays that visitors could feed since their stingers had been removed. She thought it would be a great idea for Charlotte to feed them, but Charlotte refused, and crying, she resisted her mother's efforts to put her hand in the tank. Karen decided she would go first to show her it was safe. Charlotte watched with tears in her eyes and a quivering lip as her mom grabbed some food, flattened her hand as the employees at the exhibit had instructed her, and slid it into the water. But before Karen knew it, she felt a pinch on her hand and jerked it out of the tank to discover a small cut. One of the stingrays had bit her.

They moved on from the exhibit, and Karen didn't tell Charlotte to put her hand back into the tank. But the example her mother had set for her was an important one. Karen had encouraged Charlotte to conquer her fear, but she had done something else, too: she had demonstrated that she would be with her daughter through the scary moments, she would go first, and she wouldn't ask her daughter to do anything she wasn't willing to do herself. And, most important, if something bad *did* happen, that they could handle it together.

In life, there is always the next fear to conquer and the next unknown to face. Never underestimate the value of modeling initiative and reasonable risk taking to your children. In instances like these, they can begin to test the limits of their assumptions, they can learn new information and take a controlled chance—all with your support. But they will have the confidence to do so only if they see you pave the way. If you want your kids to take risks and venture out: go first.

26

Return to the Rock

Look to the rock from which you were cut and to the quarry from which you were hewn.

—ISAIAH 51:1

As the old saying goes, if you do not know where you are from, you cannot know where you are going.

Though I was born and raised in a small town in Indiana, I have always considered my story to have begun in Ireland. My father's family goes back generations in the United States and has lived in the Midwest for decades, but my mother's family came from Ireland. I've always had a particular connection to her side. Whereas my two older brothers were named in part after my father, I was named after my mother's father, Richard Michael Cawley.

My grampa was one of six children raised in a two-room house in the rural landscape of Tubbercurry, Ireland. He left when he was seventeen years old. After crossing the Atlantic, he passed through Ellis Island in 1923 and drove a bus in Chicago for forty years. We always knew he was tough, but we never knew *how* tough until after he retired. In retirement, just to get out of the house, he signed up for a courier service delivering packages in downtown Chicago. During one delivery, as he cut through an alley, a man pointed a gun at him. So, of course, the big-knuckled seventy-year-old Irishman took a swing at the assailant before being knocked down and hearing the weapon fire as the mugger ran away.

As the story goes, my grandfather reportedly staggered out into the street, where he encountered a police officer and mentioned that his head was hurting, thinking the assailant had perhaps given him a concussion. When he arrived at a hospital, the medical team noticed a bullet hole in the back of his shirt near his neck. An X-ray revealed that a bullet had entered his head and was still inside, but the doctors decided to leave it since it would be too dangerous to remove it. Our family has told the story for decades, joking that our grandfather had been shot in the head—but all it did was make him mad.

The Bible teaches, "Look to the rock from which you were cut and to the quarry from which you were hewn" (Isaiah 51:1). I've always felt it's important to return to your roots, to go back where you came from in order to figure out who you are. After my graduation from Hanover College, I was going to do just that. My grandfather and I had been planning a trip to his homeland so I could see where he had grown up and understand my family history better. It was going to be a special journey, but sadly, we would never go together; he passed away a few months before the trip.

As my dad and I drove to Chicago for his funeral, he asked me what I was going to do about the trip to Ireland. My dad was practical and always did whatever made the most sense when it came to work and family. I said I would still go, and he surprised me by agreeing that I should, even though I was about to leave college with no job and no prospects. I think Dad knew how much my grandfather and our relationship had meant to me. He knew that there was something for me in Ireland, something I needed to find, and that I wouldn't rest until I had.

In the summer of 1981, I landed in Galway on a typically wet, cloudy Irish day. I was reunited with my Great-aunt Ann and a cousin who would travel with me over the course of the next month. I worked in Morrissey's pub in Doonbeg, which is still owned by a distant cousin, and I will never forget living above and working in an Irish pub. I poured pints of Guinness for farmers in the morning before they headed out to the fields and learned firsthand the backbreaking work of cutting and stacking turf from the bogs.

Each weekend night, I watched the pub fill to overflowing with raucous celebration as the small community came together. I had never seen anything like it, but I felt right at home. There were ten-year-old children running around underfoot, and even the local priest was there enjoying himself—with the understanding that he would see us all at Mass on Sunday morning.

In the weeks that followed, I traveled to various towns throughout the country. Finally, I made my way to Tubbercurry, the small town in northwest Ireland where my grandfather had grown up. Once there, my grandfather's sister told me she could take me to the two-room house where she and my grandfather had been raised.

We drove through the sprawling hills of the rural landscape, always lush and green in the wet climate, and pulled over onto a narrow road once we arrived at the thatch-roofed home. We walked up the muddy path to the front door, where we were greeted by the current occupants. They invited us inside to look around the small home where my grandfather had grown up with six brothers and sisters. Looking around that two-room modest home in the countryside of Ireland, my mind returned to an earlier conversation with my grandfather.

Not quite a year before, I had walked into the family room of the spacious white brick Tudor home my father had purchased after most of us had left for college. In my parents' new home that day, I found my Grampa Cawley sitting in a chair in the living room, silent, with tears in his eyes.

Surprised, I asked him what was wrong.

He looked at me with eyes that had seen more life and experienced more heartbreak than I had. "I just never thought a child of mine would ever live in a house like this," he said quietly.

I thought I understood at the time, but as we left my grandfather's boyhood home in Ireland, I could see just how far he'd come from that humble Irish home to the heart of the American dream.

Walking back to the car, I spotted a short hill across the street. I told my great-aunt I would be back in a moment and hiked up to get a better view. Standing there, I could see my grandfather's home surrounded by the rolling countryside. To the east, I could see the Ox Mountains and thought of the family legend I had heard so many times.

When my grandfather was deciding whether or not to come to America and leave his family behind, his mother told him he had to go "because there's a future there," even though it meant he wouldn't be able to see her for another twenty-five years. Standing there on that hilltop, I knew that *I* was that future and he had left everything he knew to give his children and grandchildren better opportunities. Her belief in him, and his belief in America, were a foundational principle of my life. The gratitude I feel for her and for my grandfather has never left me. When I returned to the United States after that trip, I had a newfound purpose: I wanted to be the kind of person who would make my grandfather proud, and I wanted to be the kind of father and grandfather who would one day instill the same sense of responsibility and admiration of this country into his own children and grandchildren.

Atop that hill in Ireland as a young man, I snapped a photo that would become a family heirloom. The framed picture has hung in our house for decades, along with the words of Joshua 24:15: "As for me and my house, we will serve the Lord." My children grew up with that image and verse on the wall beside the front door of almost every house in which they've ever lived. I always wanted them to know where their story began and remember the rock from which they were hewn.

In our busy culture we often don't take the time to seek out a connection with the past if it isn't immediately available to us. With genetic testing kits and online ancestry sites, we can instantly receive facts about our origins, but taking the time to search out the past is entirely different. It involves time, patience, and humility.

Years later, Karen and I wanted our children to see the country that is such an integral part of their story, as well. When I was governor of Indiana, we fulfilled that dream and took them to Ireland on a family vacation. During our travels, I wanted to return to the countryside and show them where their great-grandfather had been born. Despite my desire to do so, I had a problem: I had no idea how to find that grassy hillside.

We drove through the narrow country streets in our small European car, remembering to keep it on the left side of the road, with only my shoddy memory to use as a map. I knew the Ox

Mountains had been to the east when I had taken the picture, and other than a few details about the landscape, that was all I remembered.

As the afternoon dragged on, our search was proving to be fruitless, but then we turned a corner and went down a road with a stone fence that looked familiar to me. I stopped the car and got out, fairly certain that that was the spot.

The house that had been there was long gone, but the plot of land looked the same and had a stone fence bearing a resemblance to the one in the photo I had taken. I was almost sure it was the same place, but I couldn't be positive without climbing the hill I had scaled decades earlier.

The mood in the car was shifting as the kids began to grow bored with my efforts and dinnertime was fast approaching. We had been looking for hours, and now that this location had finally turned up, they were satisfied. It also seemed riskier to climb a fence on someone's land than it had been when I was a young man. Even though I wasn't sure it was the same place, at most of the family's insistence, I agreed to move on with our day, and we headed back into town. Before driving to our hotel, we stopped to refuel the tiny car at a gas station. My daughter Charlotte was irritated with me for not making sure that the location was the same spot I had visited in my youth, and she let me know. "Dad, we have to go back," she said.

I was reminded then how we had taught our kids never to give up, and I agreed with her. We had to go back. If we didn't, I would always wonder, and whatever I had been trying to find— and show my kids how to seek—would be lost.

As we arrived back at the area, I looked at the grassy hill to the left of the road, damp with the wet air of Ireland. I gazed to the east and saw the Ox Mountains, their gray, distant peaks looming miles away. That had to be it, but we would need to get to the top of the hill to be certain. Charlotte and I jumped out of the car and hopped the fence across the street, just as I had as a young college graduate. A cow was grazing nearby, and it was unclear on whose land we were trespassing. Karen drove the car around a bend in the road and up a steep incline to the top of the hill. Once there, I turned around and pulled out the weathered photograph to hold it up to the view. Below was clearly the same land where the house used to be, which was now being used as a cow pasture. The earth dipped slightly from the traces of my grandfather's childhood home, and the opening in the fence lined up with where an iron gate was in the photograph. It was unmistakably the same contours of the land I had looked at thirty years ago.

"I was right here," I told Charlotte.

We held the image up again to the landscape and realized that we were, indeed, looking at the rock "from which [we] were hewn."

As a young man, I had traveled to Ireland with big dreams, unsure of what the future would hold. Being there with my family, I wasn't nearly as concerned about my career achievements as I had thought I would be. Rather, I felt blessed to be there with them, to have a family that was thriving in the midst of everything else we were pursuing.

A few years later, I would return in an official role to Ireland as vice president of the United States with much fanfare and large motorcades. That time, I took my eighty-six-year-old mother with me. She and I walked the streets of Doonbeg, where both of her grandparents had grown up, and as we exited the vehicles at an official stop, she walked up to the rope line and started shaking hands with the people who had come out to see us. We had returned to the special place where both of our stories began.

People sometimes ask me what I was thinking about on inauguration day in 2017 when I took the oath of office on the western side of the Capitol building and assumed the second highest position in our government.[1] I wasn't thinking about the crowds, the cameras, or all the work that would lie ahead. I was thinking about my great-grandmother, what she had known to be true about America, and all my grandfather had given me by believing it, too.

Never give up looking for your past. Keep searching until you've seen it, walked it, and owned it. You can't really understand where you can go, and where your children can go, until you understand where you've been.

Return to the rock from which you were hewn.

27

Face Tragedy Together

Peace I leave with you; my peace I give you. I do not give to you as the world gives. Do not let your hearts be troubled and do not be afraid.

—JOHN 14:27

September 11, 2001, started out like any other day for our family, just as it did for countless families across the United States. Michael, Charlotte, and Audrey were in third grade, first grade, and kindergarten at the time. They got ready for school, brushed their teeth, put on their uniforms for their Christian school where Karen taught art part-time, and grabbed a quick breakfast. Before they piled into the car, I corralled them by the front door for a quick devotional as we all prepared to dash off to our days.

Each morning, I tried to say the Lord's Prayer and offer a Bible verse before we went our separate ways. With the busyness that is so often associated with young children's school days and work that never seems to stop, it's hard to find a moment to share in the hectic morning routine. For our family, it would often look like a rushed encounter to the protests of kids who might have been running late already. But it was important to me and Karen that we at least try to start our day together and with prayer.

That morning, as soon as we were done, everyone hurried away and the day began. Karen drove with the children to Immanuel Christian School. Their daily route took them directly past the north side of the Pentagon, the very site where the hijacking of Flight 77[1] would claim the lives of 184 people less than two hours later.[2]

Shortly after word of the terrorist attacks in New York and Washington, DC, reached the kids' school, a voice came over its PA system and announced that students would be dismissed for the rest of the day because "bombs are going off in Washington, DC." That caused panic throughout the building, as many of the students had parents who worked on Capitol Hill or at the Pentagon. Even though she hadn't heard from me, Karen decided she needed to reassure Michael, Charlotte, and Audrey and went to each of their classrooms to tell them, "Dad is okay," even though she didn't know if I was.

As I recounted in So Help Me God, after I arrived at my congressional office, a plane hit the Pentagon, just miles away in Arlington, Virginia, causing smoke to billow into the air, pouring black soot onto the canvas of what had been a beautiful blue-sky day. I was on the grounds of the Capitol and made my way to where the congressional leadership had gathered in the Capitol police chief's office, which is about half a mile away from the Capitol building. There I watched on television with other congressional members as the Twin Towers in New York City fell. We soon heard that there was yet another aircraft. It was inbound—about twelve minutes out—and headed for the Capitol. But it never reached its target. We would later hear about the heroes who had brought down that plane in Shanksville, Pennsylvania. This nation—and everyone in the Capitol that day—owes those passengers a debt we will never be able to repay.

In the midst of the chaos, I felt my BlackBerry buzzing in my pocket. I picked it up and heard my wife's voice on the other end of the line simply ask, "Michael?"

"I'm okay," I said, and we both fell silent, trying to hold back our emotion.

We were overwhelmed by the losses of the day and what the attack on American soil would mean for our country. Karen told me that if I could, it would be important for the kids to see me in person. I told her I would do my best to make my way home as soon as I could.

Karen, Michael, Charlotte, and Audrey drove home the same way they had gone to school just hours before, passing the Pentagon, where they could clearly see the devastation. A black hole smoldered in the side of the massive building—a sight they would see every day on their way to school over the next year.

As the day wore on, the unofficial meeting with congressional members in the police chief's office ended and I made my way out to the street toward my car, which was parked near the House of Representatives. The highways were closed, but I was waved through the barricades by law enforcement officials because of my congressional license plate. It was a sobering moment, driving on an empty interstate through a normally crowded, bustling city. I traveled over deserted bridges that are typically packed with traffic and finally pulled up to our home. I hurried up the steps and through the front door, where I hugged Michael, Charlotte, Audrey, and Karen, holding them close.

Karen and I thought it was important to be honest with our children about what had happened. They lived in the nation's capital now—we had brought them there—and they needed to know the reality of the situation. We gathered around the kitchen table for a family meeting. We told them that bad men had attacked our country and lives had been lost. There were even some people at their school who would be impacted. We reassured them that we would be all right but explained their dad would have to be at the Capitol working longer hours now because of the attack. We wanted them to know not only that their mom and dad were okay but that we had a role to play in this and we were following God's call to serve our country—even when it was hard. Then we prayed together for the families of the fallen, the heroes of that day, and our country and its leaders.

As I grabbed my briefcase and got ready to go back to the Capitol, I heard Audrey's voice. My youngest daughter was putting the pieces together and was worried about her dad. We had been honest with our children about what had taken place, so naturally, they had questions. As I collected my belongings, trying not to forget anything, I was distracted by her interruptions.

"Daddy?" I heard her repeatedly ask. "Daddy?"

The stress of the day caught up to me and when I turned to her, it wasn't without a bit of exasperation. "What?" I said.

Gazing up at me with her big brown eyes, she pushed her long, dark hair away from her face and asked, "If we have to make a war, do you have to go?"

That stopped me dead in my tracks.

I dropped to one knee, put my arms around my little girl, and told her that Daddy was too old. As I headed out the door, I thought of all the fathers, mothers, sons, and daughters who would answer that question differently in the months ahead. We have an immense debt of gratitude to the service members who looked into their children's eyes that day and gave a different answer, who responded to the call to serve—not because they had to but because they wanted to defend the freedom of this nation. God bless them all.

Returning to Capitol Hill, I drove back across the Theodore Roosevelt Bridge, which I had crossed earlier that day. As I drove, I looked up and saw the president's two United States Marine Corps helicopters flying at a low level over the Potomac River. The roads were still eerily vacant. I reported to the police chief's headquarters, which was located in a basement, and found a group of members listening to the voice of former governor of Pennsylvania Tom Ridge coming through a speakerphone. He would soon be named the first ever director of the Department of Homeland Security, and served as secretary of homeland security in President George W. Bush's administration after the department was created. He told us what they knew—that the people who had attacked the United States wanted to hit us again and do so even worse.[3]

I looked around at all of the Republicans and Democrats in that basement, some on folding chairs, others seated on the floor or leaning against the walls. At some point, a decision was made that we would convene a press conference on the steps of the US Capitol, and a prayer was said before we departed.

At the press conference, it was less important what was said than it was that we were there. We were showing Americans—and our enemies—that we hadn't left our post, that the country's leaders would stay no matter what. The decision presaged my response to the events of another tragic day, one that would take place in the Capitol building two decades later.

At the end of the press conference, someone started singing "God Bless America," and everyone joined in. It was a surprising moment of grace. Republicans, Democrats, and I think some reporters all sang together, united as one voice. It was an encouragement to us at the close of a long and tragic day, but it was a comfort to the nation, too.

That was solidified for me a few weeks later when I was home in my district in Indiana. I had traveled home to hold a town hall meeting with constituents to brief them on what we knew and the nation's response to the attacks. After I answered attendees' questions and we were wrapping up the event, two longtime supporters of mine, Carla and Doug Horn, came up to me. Carla wanted to tell me that their family had been encouraged by the scene of lawmakers gathered at the Capitol on that fateful day.

The Horns have five daughters, and on September 11, they were far away from their home and children. When they heard what had happened, they raced back to their family farm. Carla told me that as they had pulled up that afternoon, one of their daughters had hurried out of the house to tell them that everything was okay, "because we just saw Congressman Pence on television. And he was singing."

September 11, 2001, was a dark day in the life of our nation, but it was one of the days when I felt especially confirmed in our decision to move our family to Washington, DC. Because my family was there with me, I was able to be with them during a time of great turmoil. Even though DC seemed to be an increasingly dangerous place, I have always believed—and conveyed to our children—that the safest place to be is in the center of God's will, and I knew it was His will for us to be there together.

Like families all over the country, our little family came together that day to grieve the tragedy, to pray for the lost, and to hold one another close.

When it feels as though the future is unknown, remember God is in control, hold your family close and face tragedies and hardships *together*.

28

Encourage One Another

*Therefore encourage one another and build each other
up, just as in fact you are doing.*

—1 THESSALONIANS 5:11

Years ago, a pastor told me that "everybody is underencouraged." I found that insight to be profound, and I've taken it
to heart. In my public life, especially when it comes to my staff
and constituents, I've seen so many instances when a mere pat on
the back changed someone's day—including mine.

The fall of 2006 was a particularly trying time during my
service in Congress. I was working on immigration reform and
believed that despite years of failure and inaction from Washington, we could find a solution to the growing problem of illegal immigrants entering the United States. Though the situation
at our southern border had gotten worse, as the grandson of an
Irish immigrant, I've always known that our country is a nation
of immigrants and benefits from people coming here to make
America their home. The seventeenth-century economist Adam
Smith argued that no nation grows but by population.[1] But welcoming people here legally is the only way to do it. I believed it
could be done then—and I still do.

In the midst of the ongoing crisis, I came across an idea proposed by a Colorado rancher named Helen Krieble. She suggested to me that we could create a guest worker program and allow people to apply outside the country to live and work here. I worked with Senator Kay Bailey Hutchison of Texas to develop the Pence-Hutchison proposal. I thought it could be a bipartisan solution to an issue that Americans wanted Washington to fix. But that bipartisanship on a contested issue didn't win me any popularity points. Hard-line Republicans said it was equivalent to amnesty, while those on the political left argued that it was cruel to require people to apply outside the country to work in the United States. With both sides attacking me, I knew we were onto something, and I felt compelled to keep going.

By the summer of 2006, our efforts started getting the attention of leaders in Washington, but I was surprised one day when my staff informed me that I had been invited to the Oval Office to meet with President George W. Bush.

As I arrived at the West Wing, I waited outside the historic room, trying to make small talk with the president's secretary as I nervously waited to be called in. The door opened, and a member of Bush's staff welcomed me inside. Portraits of distinguished American heroes lined the walls and seemed to train their gaze on me. The president, Vice President Dick Cheney, and other members of the administration were in the room. Over the course of the next hour, Bush, wearing his signature cowboy boots, sat in front of the fireplace as I pitched our proposal from one of the historic yellow couches. The president knew the details of our immigration plan and asked me questions for more than an hour. At the end of the meeting he stood up and put his hand on my shoulder. "Mike, I know you're taking a lot of heat, and I asked you here because I just wanted you to be encouraged," he said.

"Thank you, Mr. President," I said.

"No, really, Mike," he pressed. "I wanted you to get some encouragement. I'd like you to see me as an encourager."

With that I held up my hand and said with a chuckle, "Mr. President, for a small-town boy from southern Indiana to have the opportunity to meet with the leader of the free world . . . I'm encouraged."

He let out his hearty Texan laugh and nodded. "Good," he said, slapping me on the back, and I made my way to the door.

I've carried the lesson of that moment with me for many years. When I meet young people on the road who are involved in politics, I try to encourage them with the words "It's going to be your turn soon." They usually respond with a smile, secretly hoping that it will be. They are eager to enter the arena, grab the baton, and go. I want them to know that if they follow their dreams, it won't be long before they are the ones on the campaign trail championing their values, speaking at events, and offering words of inspiration and hope to the American people. I can always tell how much it means to them to be reminded of this.

We all have passions that we're energized to commit to. But often the work of getting there is hard and thankless. So be encouraged—and keep encouraging others. You don't have to do so in a public manner, but little words of confidence to your family, staff, or coworkers will go a long way. It's easy for people to assume that they are falling short if they don't hear otherwise, and a simple reminder that they are doing well can make all the difference. You can never encourage others too much, especially when they're going against the tide.

So be an encourager, give encouragement, and remember: everyone is underencouraged.

29

Let Your Kids Ride

Do you give the horse its strength or clothe its neck with a flowing mane?

—JOB 39:19

My love of horses started at a young age. For my second birthday, I asked for a cake with horses and a corral atop the icing, and a photo of that day shows a crew-cut boy smiling from ear to ear, thrilled with the outcome. When we were teenagers, my brothers and I helped clear land for a hundred head of cattle where my father built a barn that became home to two quarter horses. The area was roughly one hundred acres, and it was hard work. Despite the toil, that field was where my real love affair with horses started, and I wanted my children to have the same admiration of these gentle beasts.

Our three kids sat a horse before they were two years old. We would take them to a little ranch in Indiana and give them a chance to ride, even just for a short walk around the arena to get used to being in the saddle. Our family has taken the opportunity to ride on horseback any chance we get, and we benefited from friends who had horses. Greg Garrison, the esteemed lawyer who prosecuted Mike Tyson and later took over my radio show, would let Michael, Charlotte, and Audrey ride his horses in the field across from his home. Greg and his wife, Phyllis, frequently welcomed our family to their house. The kids were in awe of the rustic decor and always got a kick out of Greg's cowboy demeanor. They helped get the horses ready to go by brushing their silky coats, loading up the saddles, and climbing up to get the stirrups fitted and the reins tied just right. Even in freezing snow or blistering heat, they were ready to ride.

When Audrey was only seven years old, she rode a twenty-year-old paint-striped horse named King George at the Garrisons' ranch. We walked the horses to the edge of the property and crossed a street to get to the open range where the kids could let loose.

When we were trotting through the field, King George, who was very gentle with children, took off across the grass.

Audrey looked like a natural as the animal cantered with her across the landscape. Even though they were racing away from us, I didn't panic. I knew she was safe with him—not only because he was a good horse and would be careful not to lose her but because I knew she was comfortable riding. She was confident—horses will do that for you—and so we let her run.

A horse isn't easy to control. It takes backbone to command the animal and lead it in the direction you want it to go in. I taught my kids to have a sense of respect for horses, so that the massive animals would respect them in return. But I also taught them how to take charge. Once the kids knew how to balance those two principles, I could let them run free.

Horses always find their way back to the barn, and when they sense they're headed in the direction of home, they move a lot faster. Charlotte discovered that as a child. One year, as our ride was ending, her horse sensed that the barn was nearby. The animal took off racing, heading toward the busy street. Charlotte took control and calmed the horse down, but it was a lesson of a different kind. Horses are ready to venture out, to ride away from their comfortable dwelling, but they will still run to their barn when it is time to go home.

When our children were little, I would set them down in front of me on the horse. We would ride together, their small frames tucked up next to me and safe inside my arms as I took the reins. But I knew they would outgrow that arrangement and would need to know how to take control when they were riding solo.

The Bible says, "Train up a child in the way he should go; even when he is old he will not depart from it" (Proverbs 22:6).

We have to train our kids to deal with difficult situations, knowing that we won't always be there to get them out of harm's way. Riding horses isn't for everyone, so find other opportunities for your children to practice their independence. Teach them the most important things, and then let them explore new territory on their own. It's hard to put our children into positions where we know they could fall and get hurt. But if we don't hand over the reins, they'll never learn how to take the lead in their lives.

Train your kids in the way they should go; then let them ride.

30

When You're There, Be There

*My dear brothers and sisters, take note of this: Every-
one should be quick to listen.*

—JAMES 1:19

On September 11, 2001, I was serving in my first year in
Congress. I found myself on Capitol Hill in the wake of
the attack on New York City and the Pentagon and the heroism
that took place in the skies over Shanksville, Pennsylvania. As the
day unfolded, I made my way to the Capitol police chief's office,
where I was surrounded by the Republican and Democrat leaders of the House and Senate. We were receiving regular briefings
from security officials and, along with the rest of the country,
were watching the tragic events unfold on the television screen
in the office. Due to the sheer volume of people attempting to
make calls in our nation's capital, the cell phone towers were paralyzed, but I was still receiving news bulletins and texts on my
BlackBerry.[1]

After I was elected to Congress in 2000, our office learned
of a new phone called a BlackBerry that could be used to
send emails and receive updates on the news. Since my chief
of staff lived and worked in Indiana and my family and I lived

in Washington, DC, our office acquired one for him and one for me so we could stay in communication. We used it to share notes, updates, and the occasional news article with each other but it wasn't a significant part of my day. Its role in my life and the lives of others, however, would soon become much more prevalent.

Standing in the Capitol police chief's office that day, I read some of the news reports I was receiving out loud to the small group gathered there. Several of the senior members of the House and Senate, who were unable to use their cell phones, huddled around me and asked why my BlackBerry was still working. The chief of police explained that the devices worked differently than voice calls. They were able to continue operating because they used a data system that was separate from the phone system's. People inside the World Trade Center were also able to use the handheld devices to reach the outside world.[2]

It was a harrowing day that changed our country forever, but it prompted a shift in the way Congress, and in many ways our society, would interact in the months and years ahead. Post-9/11, Congress went on to distribute BlackBerrys to every member of Congress,[3] changing the way those in our nation's capital communicated.[4] Within a few short years, more than eight thousand elected officials and staff in Washington were using BlackBerrys on a daily basis. It was the first time such a device was widely used in the halls of our government.

How does all of this relate to putting your family first?

In the previous chapters, I encouraged you to go home for dinner. Physically being with your family, however, doesn't necessarily mean you are engaged with them. Shortly after those momentous days in September 2001, my BlackBerry underwent a transformation. At first, it was an easy way to stay connected with work and family. If my children or Karen called during the day, I would always answer, even if I was busy. I'd often listen to one of my kids for a while before they asked what I was doing.

"I'm in a meeting," I'd answer, and they would hurriedly reply that they could speak to me another time. But they were more important than anything that needed to be done at work. If they called, I answered. And they knew I would always pick up the phone.

However, though my BlackBerry was immensely useful on September 11th, and in other pivotal moments when I needed to be reachable, the phone quickly became a distraction. Alerts, emails, and text messages only got more intrusive as time went by. When our kids were still at home, my BlackBerry often lit up with a message from a staff member or a news alert.

So Karen and I established another rule to help me mentally disconnect from the constant demands of the job. When I was home, I wanted to really be home. We had a little crystal dish that sat on the piano by the front door of our house in Arlington, Virginia, where we lived during my last years in Congress. When I arrived home from the Capitol each night after a long day, I put my BlackBerry into the dish. If I forgot to do so, Karen was quick to remind me. "Phone in the dish," she would say.

Putting the phone out of reach was a small habit, but the meaning behind it goes back to the general idea of prioritizing family over work. Whatever messages were coming in could wait until I had heard about how one of our kids had done on a test or what frustrations and highlights Karen had experienced that day as a teacher. If there was an emergency, I could always be reached another way.

In short, I not only made sure I was home for dinner whenever I could be, but I took the steps to be mentally present, too.

Let me just say that I know this is increasingly difficult to do in a world where cell phones seem to be omnipresent and entertainment and information can be reached at the touch of a screen. I wanted to set an example for my children of how to use a device without letting it consume their attention. In an ironic twist, they are often the ones reminding me to do this today. Even if my screen is out of reach, my adult kids will let me know that they can tell my mind has wandered to something work related. I still need to make an effort to focus on the people around me, so I know how hard it can be when there is something on the sidelines demanding your attention. But your family deserves your full attention. And it doesn't matter if we create the time and space to sit at the table together if we spend the majority of that time in a state of distraction.

You might be able to come up with a different "dish," a way you can put the demands of your job out of reach while you are with family. Maybe everyone in the family can practice putting their devices in a separate location before coming to the dinner table, or you can establish a period of time each night when phones are not used so you can all focus on one another.

When you're there, be there. Put the phone in the dish.

31

Swim in the Creek

He leads me beside still waters. He restores my soul.

—PSALM 23:2–3

After being elected to Congress in the fall of 2000, Karen and I bought a ranch-style home nestled on a single street in rural Indiana. The house sat in a small neighborhood right in the middle of the countryside with farmland stretching for miles. The little three-bedroom house tended to gather dust and a few mice caught in traps when we would walk in the door after being away in Washington. The soybean fields over the fence in the backyard were so lit up at night with fireflies in the summertime that we dubbed the small rise in the land "Firefly Mountain." I used to tell people that I could see six miles and count eighteen barns from my back porch, and that was just one of the things that made it feel like home.

When we moved into that house, I learned that the neighborhood was next to a stretch of the Flatrock River, which runs through the southern part of our state. As soon as I learned that the Flatrock was so close to our house, I decided to get the kids down to the water as soon as possible. I wanted them to experience something I had loved about growing up in Indiana:

swimming in Haw Creek every day of those long, hot summers. Our kids had grown up in concrete pools in Indianapolis and Virginia, and I thought it was time for them to experience Indiana as I knew it.

On the first Saturday after we moved, I told the kids we had to check out the river, so we put on swimsuits and old tennis shoes, packed up towels and a cooler with drinks and sandwiches, and headed down the road to a grassy field that led to the water's edge. We traversed the open grass, making sure to keep out of the backyards of our neighbors, until we came to a wooded area where we could hear trickling water just beyond the trees. Climbing over fallen limbs and dodging branches, we finally arrived at the banks of the mighty Flatrock River.

The water, flowing over rocks and wooden logs, was dirt brown, and the river was more of a creek in its width and depth. It would be possible to get to the other side, but the current was faster and the water deeper farther from the shore. We could see the bottom of the creek just off the muddy beach where we stood, our shoes sinking into the slimy, wet mud. Once deeper, there would be no way to see the bottom, even in its shallow parts. But I knew they could handle it.

Standing on the shoreline, our three kids looked up at me, with questions in their eyes, as if to ask "You want us to swim in *that*?"

I assured them that they were going to love it and reminded them to keep their old tennis shoes on when they went in. Slowly they made their way into the water, squealing with surprise and delight at the cold temperature. It wasn't long until they were splashing and jumping, testing out the limits of their new playground. They made their way to a large tree with exposed roots in the middle of the creek and climbed up onto it. I went in after them, grabbing a rusted slat from a metal fence and plunging it into the dirt surrounding the roots. We dubbed the small landmass "Treasure Island." And that was it. They were hooked.

From that day forward, they never turned down an opportunity to get into the Flatrock, riding their bikes every day of the summer to get there. They pedaled through the neighborhood to where the concrete ended and started up again, speeding down the hill to gain momentum and make it across the field. The muddy water quickly became a place for their make-believe worlds, dreams, and memories.

I wanted them to swim in the creek—not just for the fun of playing in the river but for the experience of getting their clothes dirty and shoes muddy and ending the day worn out after looking for crawdads and letting their imaginations run wild. I wanted them to overcome the trepidation that so easily comes when children don't have the opportunity to take a few risks in their own backyard.

You don't need to have access to a muddy riverbed to show your kids how to be comfortable with being uncomfortable. Demonstrating what you loved as a child isn't always possible, either, but getting your kids away from their usual activities is important. Convey the joy you found in your treasured childhood explorations.

Inspire your kids to adventure, and swim in the creek.

32

Have a Family Night

*Train up a child in the way he should go; even when he
is old he will not depart from it.*

—PROVERBS 22:6

When Karen and I first got married, we talked about how
we wanted to raise our kids with biblical principles. After
our kids reached an age where they were old enough to appreciate
a little Bible study, we looked for a way to carve out regular family
devotional time. Around that same time, we came across a book
by Focus on the Family called *An Introduction to Family Nights*,
which included Bible lessons and games. With its discovery, a tradition was born.

Every Friday night, we came together for a Bible lesson,
complete with a game or skit, and I always came up with a catchy
or corny slogan to help the kids better remember the lesson.

Inside the front flap of the book, I began to record our "Family Nights," with the date and slogan written next to brief notes
about the night. The earliest entry is from January 1998, when
Michael was six years old, Charlotte was four, and Audrey was
three. Sometimes there is a Bible verse written down that was
incorporated into the nightly lesson, and the entry for January

2003 includes a sketch of the US Capitol, for reasons I can no longer remember.

One of our favorite games was "You need a cross to get across." For that game, I spread white flour on the cement floor of our basement in the shape of a cross and the kids tried to step only on the flour as they crossed from one side of the floor to the other—an impossible task. It was a helpful illustration of how we are separated from God because of our sins and we need the cross of Jesus Christ to reach Him.

Beside the entry for "If Mom is great, appreciate" is a list of items detailing what each of our children appreciated about their mom. Next to Audrey's name is "cat Mommy gave to me," Michael's includes "lizard—day went to [Virginia] and bagels," and Charlotte's has the words "gerbil (I'm her Mommy) and baby doll." Parents, take note: more than almost anything else you'll do for them, children remember and appreciate the pets you bring into their home.

Other slogans I made up for the lessons were "Might be strange, but God don't change," "Play together, stay together," and "Just like air, God is there." "I can say I'm made of clay" was another one, along with "Faith in Christ, new light" and "Before the fall, He made it all." These catchphrases may seem silly, but our children remembered them for years to come. And they helped Karen and me distill the lessons of God's goodness and often appreciate them anew. Since we incorporated those lessons into our family early on, they prepared our children for when they would need to rely on these age-old biblical truths.

Spending time together as a family on Friday nights isn't exactly a novel idea. Unbeknownst to us at the time, the tradition had been going on for thousands of years. It didn't occur to me until several years later that the act of getting together at the end of the week for reflection on scripture, fellowship, and a meal was like the Jewish tradition of the Shabbat dinner. I would never compare my catchphrases, silly skits, and Papa Johns deliveries to that sacred practice, but the similarities struck me later in life. I felt as though God had led our little family to a tradition that had strengthened families for thousands of years.

Years later, Karen and I were honored to attend Shabbat dinners in Jerusalem with our children and in the home of close friends in Indiana. We cherished those evenings when we participated in the kosher meal and took part in the tradition of breaking off a piece of bread from a single, shared loaf. As I sat at those special gatherings, my mind would drift back to our three little kids sitting on the floor of our living room listening to a Bible lesson before digging into pizza. Though there are differences in the two evenings, the concept is the same: break bread together at the end of every week, open the scripture. Essentially, go home for dinner.

Proverbs 22:6 says, "Train up a child in the way he should go; even when he is old he will not depart from it." To this day, my now-adult children can still recite many of the silly sayings from those Family Nights with a smile and an eye roll. They are fun memories, but they served a deeper purpose; they conveyed invaluable spiritual lessons that we wanted our children to remember when they were older and no longer under our care.

Establishing a way to have fun together and learn important lessons can be done in other ways. You don't have to order pizza and play games every weekend to connect with your children. But dedicating time to be together every week helps you grow closer as a family.

Make one night a week "Family Night." Teach your children "the way [they] should go," and have fun doing it.

33

Practice Integrity

The integrity of the upright guides them.

During my first term in Congress, my chief of staff established a rule that applied to anyone who worked at the front desk and answered the phone. If I was in the office but wasn't able to speak to someone who called, our staff was supposed to say that I "wasn't available" instead of saying that I "wasn't in." The two phrases have a minor difference that might seem unimportant. But there is a major distinction between the two of them: one is the truth, and one is not.

There are times when it might have been awkward for our staff to relay that message, but creating a culture of honesty in our office was important. Telling the truth is directly related to living with integrity, and nothing could be more important in public service than that. We expected everyone to abide by that standard, including me. And I tried to live up to that standard even if others didn't quite understand.

One evening, I was driving home from the Capitol after a long day of votes and meetings. Without paying attention, I accidentally entered the high-occupancy vehicle (HOV) lane.

I saw a few police cars up ahead, and it occurred to me that the clock had long since struck five, the time when the regular lane I had been using turned into an HOV lane. There was only one person in my car—me—which meant that I was in the wrong place.

I passed the police cars, which had pulled over several motorists in front of me, and positioned my car on the shoulder of the highway in front of the squad cars. I put my car in park and waited. After a few minutes, one of the officers approached my vehicle, and I rolled down the window.

"Hi, there," he said, with a confused look on his face. "Did I pull you over?"

"No, sir," I answered.

"Did he?" he asked, pointing to the other car.

"No, sir," I said again. "I just realized that I was in the wrong lane."

He nodded slowly and walked back to where his car was parked in front of the other cop car. A few moments went by, and he came back to my little silver Chevy Malibu. I rolled down the window a second time.

"I didn't pull you over?" he asked again.

"No," I tried to explain. "I lost track of the time and didn't realize I was in the HOV lane."

"Neither of us pulled you over?" he asked again.

"No."

"Well, we're not going to give you a ticket," he said. "We don't get people pulling themselves over very often."

"Thank you, Officer," I replied.

"One more thing," he said, motioning to my official license plate. "Are you a congressman?"

"Yes, sir. From Indiana."

"Yeah," he said, shaking his head slightly. "I thought all you politicians were supposed to be dishonest."

I shrugged, not sure what to say, and he waved me along.

It was a small act of honesty that I easily could have avoided. But I've always believed that the little things are the big things, that the decisions we make in the small, seemingly insignificant moments matter just as much as those we make in the big moments.

Our office policy of always telling the truth might have appeared excessive, but culture is created through the habits that we encourage or discourage in others. Requiring honesty of my staff meant that I had to live by the same rules. It also gave the impression to our team, our constituents, and the media that the truth was important to us. They could rely on that.

This is a good way to operate in a relationship, too. When we're honest with our spouse, it creates a strong foundation of trust. I often find myself sharing details with Karen that might prove to be trivial, but I don't want them to be revealed later, when it might look as though I was trying to keep something from her.

Develop a habit of honesty. I say a habit, because it's easier to be truthful with the big things when you're consistently honest about the small things. The Bible says, "Jesus grew in wisdom and stature, and in favor with God and man" (Luke 2:52). Prepare now to be the person you want to be in the future, when more will be required of you. Whenever you can, choose to be truthful, even when it seems as though it isn't important. You cannot expect to be able to run a race without training in the months leading up to the event. The same is true of the trials you will face.

When tests arrive, as they do for everyone, you will be who you prepared to be in the quiet moments before then, the moments when no one was watching and your actions didn't seem to matter. You never know when you will be called upon to take a stand, so use the small, seemingly minor occurrences to get ready.

Prepare your heart, be honest, and practice integrity.

34

Carry Your Children

There you saw how the Lord your God carried you, as a father carries his son, all the way you went until you reached this place.

—DEUTERONOMY 1:31

When my son, Michael, was about three years old, I had a not-so-brilliant idea.

It was 1994, and the Inaugural Brickyard 400 race was going to take place at the Indianapolis Motor Speedway.[1] I decided I would take young Michael to that massive event and create a special day for a boy and his dad. As we arrived, we joined the massive crowds of people swarming the entrance to the grounds. The racetrack of the Indianapolis Motor Speedway is a two-and-a-half-mile oval that spans more than a mile from corner to corner.[2]

The Brickyard takes place in early August, and summertime in Indiana can be scorching hot.[3] The humidity combined with the blazing sun might have prompted other people to stay home. But not Hoosiers. The place was packed for the first ever Brickyard 400, which would be the first NASCAR race to take place at the Speedway. That year, it had the highest number of attendees of any NASCAR event, with more than 250,000 people taking part.

After parking the car outside the track, I thought that my energetic son and I could walk to our seats. I don't know what I was thinking.

Michael and I had barely made it to the infield, walking on the ramp between the first and second turns to get to the inner part of the oval, when I looked down to see the little guy quickly running out of steam. I wiped the sweat from my brow and pulled out our tickets to see where we were seated. My heart sank. Our seats were on the other side of the track—over a mile away. I looked down at my young son, who was holding tightly to my hand in the commotion of people. There was no way his tiny legs were going to be able to make the trek across the grounds to the other side.

So I did what any dad would do: I stuck the tickets into my pocket, adjusted my ball cap, and hoisted him onto my shoulders. I carried him the entire way to our seats. It wasn't a particularly enjoyable experience, and the whole time, I kept thinking how ridiculous it had been to bring a three-year-old to an outdoor event like that in the sweltering heat. I never imagined how often I would happily remember that day in the years to come.

Once we got to the grandstand, we made our way to our seats and watched the race together. I pointed out the cars to him as they sped past us. Our fellow spectators had radios blasting and coolers filled with beverages, ready to enjoy the day. Michael was enthralled by the spectacle. And I took it all in, realizing that it was a memory I would always treasure. When it was all over, I picked him up, positioned him on my shoulders, and walked all the way back to our car on the other side of the track.

Jeff Gordon was the winner of the Brickyard that first year

and would win five more races in the future.[4] He lived in Indiana as a teenager and has always been a fan favorite for Hoosiers. It was a special moment for people all across Indiana to witness the first stock car speed across the finish line at the Speedway— and to see a hometown boy get the prize. But the high point of my day wasn't watching that multicolored number 24 car bring home the win;[5] it was a brown-haired boy sitting on my shoulders, joining me for the ride.

The day was hard for Michael even without walking across the infield of the track. It was hot, noisy, and a little scary. But when I carried him, it taught both of us something important: it showed me I could take my young son places even when it wasn't convenient. We could have given up and gone home, but if we had, that memory, which is so dear to me now, would have been lost. And it proved to Michael that he could get where he wanted to go, even as a toddler, with some help from his dad.

Carrying your children doesn't mean fighting their battles for them. But when we carry them through the hard moments, we set an example for how God will carry them through the storms of life.

Deuteronomy 1:31 says, "There you saw how the Lord your God carried you, as a father carries his son, all the way you went until you reached this place."

Today, my son is a fighter pilot in the Marine Corps and married with two young daughters of his own. Even though I can no longer physically carry him, I hope the memory of that day reminds him of the help that is always close at hand.

So in your family, never miss a chance to lift up those little ones around you, to show them an example of their "ever-present help in trouble" (Psalm 46:1).

Carry your children.

35

Find a Furry Friend

The righteous care for the needs of their animals.

—PROVERBS 12:10

If there's one thing I know, it's that everyone needs a pet in their life.

I've always been a pet person—from my childhood, all the way through the present day where my dog, Harley, often interrupts my work to be let out and run wild in the backyard of our home.

There's something about having a pet that glues a family together. And on an individual level, they certainly keep you humble. It's nearly impossible to clean up after a pet's mess on the kitchen floor and take yourself too seriously in other areas of life.

Harley came into my life as a Father's Day surprise when I was serving my first year as vice president. Karen had asked me what I wanted for Father's Day and I had told her, "A motorcycle." So I named him "Harley." Our beagle, Maverick, had passed away while we were on the campaign trail in 2016. The little Australian shepherd puppy looked like a ball of fluff as he was let out into the living room. I was shocked but thrilled. Karen had convinced me that we would be getting two cats since she didn't want to take care of another dog. But the kids knew I needed one. The Vice President's Residence sits on twelve acres of land, and the grounds often feel as though they're located in the middle of the country rather than Washington, DC. The land was made for a herding breed like Harley. As I took the puppy on his first walk around the yard, Karen looked at Charlotte with tears in her eyes, and said, "He has a friend." She was right.

My love of dogs began when I was a kid and continued as an adult. Proverbs 12:10 says, "The righteous care for the needs of their animals." I learned about caring for animals from my family. Growing up, we had a poodle named Poughie (pronounced "Poofy"). Our family of four boys and two girls loved her, but as the years wore on and we got older, so did she. There came a point when my parents felt that Poughie's time was coming to a close. She had lost all bladder control and had to stay in a pen in the garage most of the time. Our parents tried to prepare us for the inevitable fact that Poughie wouldn't last long, but my brothers and I would hear none of it. We told them she was fine, if just a little bit messy.

Poughie had been a constant in our lives ever since I could remember. My parents had brought her home to the first house we lived in when I was just a toddler. Dad was allergic to pet hair, so the compromise was that we could get a poodle. It was an amusing scene: we were a family of four young boys before my sisters came along, and our roughhousing did not exactly match getting a poodle for a pet. But we loved her. She was all of thirty-five pounds and the friendliest ball of black curly fur. She followed us into the woods while we played army and stayed by our side through wind, snow, sun, and rain. When I was older and getting ready to leave the house for my junior prom, clad in my baby blue tuxedo, she saw me off and my mom snapped a picture of the two of us on the front porch.

One day we got home from school to find Poughie gone. Our dad had taken her in to the veterinarian in Columbus and left her there with instructions to put her down the next morning if he didn't call. He wanted to sleep on it, but he was fairly certain that it was her time. But we boys had a different idea.

After dinner, my younger brother and I drove across town to the vet's office. We ran up to the door and pounded on it until somebody came out from the back. The office was closed, but the person was likely doing some last-minute rounds with the animals and saw the serious looks on our faces.

My brother stared directly at the worker and said, "We're here for our dog."

After we were let inside, we went straight to the back, pulled Poughie out of her cage, and took her home.

I was sure that my father would be furious, since we had openly defied him.

But when we got home, he just looked at us without saying much, and I could see that he was touched. He didn't get angry. He saw how much we cared for Poughie.

She wouldn't make it much longer, and that winter she passed away. But I never forgot the impact she made on my life.

Years later, when Karen and I were first married, another furry friend came into my life. Though I would eventually quit drinking, my favorite beer at the time was Budweiser, always in longneck bottles. During our first Christmas as a married couple, I received lots of Budweiser-themed presents from family and friends, including cozies, T-shirts, and a dartboard. The night was winding down when my new bride went into the other room and came back holding a tiny black puppy, a cocker spaniel–Labrador mix. She placed the puppy in my arms and said, "This Bud's for you," quoting the famous commercial. Everyone wanted to know what I was going to name the little pup, and I answered, of course, "Budweiser."

Bud was in our lives from that point on. She was there for our first major moves and life events. Every time we brought one of our kids home from the hospital, I remember holding the baby carrier down so she could sniff the newborn inside, her tail wagging, always the calm and peaceful animal that our kids would grow to know and love. She was unfailingly patient with children.

When we made the decision to run for Congress a third time, we moved back to my hometown and Bud came with us. After I was elected, we took her to Washington, DC, too, but by that point she was fifteen years old and moving slow.

One day while I was back in Indiana doing rounds as a new congressman, Karen looked out the window of our rental home in DC and saw a couple picking up Bud and placing her in their car. She had fallen down the hill on the side of the house and lost her collar, so they didn't know who her owners were. Karen ran out of the house and told them Bud was our dog. Then she loaded the kids into the car and drove to the vet, who told us that Bud had had a massive heart attack and needed to be put down.

One of the most heartbreaking moments of my life was sitting on the back porch of my mom's house in Indiana listening to my family, one after the other, say goodbye to Bud over the phone. I was traveling at the time and had a break in between official stops. I could hear Karen holding back tears six hundred miles away as that special dog left our life. When Bud was gone, I hung up and wiped tears away before heading to my next event.

Some people debate whether animals go to heaven. But I have a feeling they do. God promises that everything necessary for our happiness is waiting in heaven, so I just know that Bud will be there.

There are lots of reasons why having pets is good for a family. They help teach responsibility, patience, and kindness. But I think it is even deeper than that. They burrow their way into our hearts and teach us about ourselves. They complete a family and warm a home in ways that people alone just can't.

When our daughter Charlotte picked out her cat in fourth grade, she went to pet store after pet store every Sunday until she found the perfect new addition to our family: an orange-and-white cat named Pickle. The cat was traumatized by living in a house with ten other cats. I remember Charlotte pulling Pickle out of the cage at the pet store and holding her close as Pickle reached up her paw to claw at Charlotte's face. As the months went on and Pickle continued to scratch Charlotte, I told her that if the cat didn't stop, we would have to take her back. Determined not to let that happen, Charlotte held the animal's paws together when she held her until Pickle learned not to scratch. That orange-and-white cat became one of the friendliest, most loving cats you'd ever meet, and it was all because Charlotte didn't give up on her. She also had a rabbit named Marlon Bundo who lived with us at the Vice President's Residence and would go on to become a bit of a sensation after Charlotte and Karen published three children's books about him.

Animals change you, but you also learn a lot about your family members by seeing them interact with pets. I learned what caring and nurturing kids I had as I watched them care for those little creatures.

Pickle lived a long time, but she grew increasingly frail at the Vice President's Residence years later. One night late in 2019, we called Charlotte, who was living in Los Angeles, to tell her that the cat was reaching the end. That night, we put Pickle's bed next to ours in our room and woke up the next morning to find that she had passed. She is one of two of our pets buried at the Naval Observatory, the other being Audrey's little black-and-white cat, Oreo.

The Vice President's Residence has a family garden the Bidens installed when they lived there. Several stones make up a circular area surrounded by plants and flowering bushes. Listed on the pavement stones are the names of the family members and spouses of each vice president who lived at the home, along with the years of their service. In the outer area of the garden, there are small stones that would be easy to miss. They list the names of the pets that lived there, the animals that blessed the lives of each of the families, including ours.

On a small stone off to the side are the names of Harley, our cat, Hazel, Marlon Bundo, Oreo . . . and Pickle. Pets enrich our families in so many ways. So find yourself a furry friend.

36

Let the Kids Put Up the Decorations

We will not hide them from their children, but tell to the coming generation the glorious deeds of the Lord.

—PSALM 78:4

We were serving in Congress, and it had been a long week. We had made the ten-hour drive home to Indiana for the holidays, and just as we arrived in our hometown of Columbus, our minivan broke down. Karen and I decided to strike out the next day and search for an affordable minivan to replace our clunker. We not only needed a car while we were in town but needed one that could get us all back to Washington when the break was over.

Christmas was just a few days away, but anyone visiting our home wouldn't have known it. Although we usually loved getting into the holiday spirit, our family was just too busy that year. Our bags were only half unpacked from the trip, there were no decorations displayed, and many presents were still in the closet waiting to be wrapped.

The next morning, we left the kids, who were preteens at

the time, at the house and told them we'd be back that evening, likely with a new van. Hours later, we found a used replacement in our price range.

By the time we drove through the Hoosier countryside, the sun had set. We could see Christmas lights hung on the bushes and wrapped around the trees in the front yards of virtually every rural home, giving a colored glow to those dark country roads. We admired the scenes but knew our house couldn't match them. We liked making Christmas special for our children, but that year, we were resigned to just get through it.

As we turned down our street, we couldn't see our home, which was the last one on the block. Virtually every house on our street was bright with colored lights, Nativity scenes, and inflated Christmas characters. We were ready to pull into a depressing scene, a darkened home that looked as though no one lived there, but we arrived to an array of multicolored lights.

To our astonishment, the plain front of our rural ranch-style home was decorated for Christmas! A wreath was hung on the brick wall next to our front porch, candles were in each window, and lights had been haphazardly thrown onto the bushes and solitary tree in the front yard. And a lit Christmas tree was visible through the living room window. It wasn't perfect, but it was exactly what we needed.

My eyes filled with tears, and I looked at Karen, who was also overcome by emotion. We walked in the front door and our kids greeted us, all smiles. The homemade stockings were draped over the bookcase, the Nativity set was on the coffee table, and the box of ornaments was open and ready to be hung. Our eyes still wet with tears of pride, we listened as they explained what had happened while we were away. Michael had gathered the girls together and told them that Mom and Dad were dealing with a lot and so they were going to decorate the house before we got home. Despite the obstacles, they didn't let Christmas not be Christmas.

Keeping traditions is how we mark special moments. It wouldn't have ruined Christmas for us if there had been no lights or decorations, but it would have been a moment of tradition we would have missed. In the end, we get only a limited number of holidays with our families at home. These special moments matter because they show our family that gathering together matters. It's a way of carving out time together in an otherwise busy season.

Maybe hanging lights on your home isn't what makes a holiday special for your family—after all, the pressure of decorating can be a source of stress on its own. But we all have traditions that mark occasions and set them apart from other times of the year. What makes them meaningful is our willingness to keep doing them.

Whatever traditions you have, maintain them. Teach your kids to cherish them. And sometimes when life isn't easy and you can't keep up, let them put up the decorations.

37

Train Together

A cord of three strands is not quickly broken.

—ECCLESIASTES 4:12

Training for an athletic event inspires confidence, requires stamina, and teaches perseverance. And doing it with another person can prepare the two of you for life's challenges. As the Bible teaches, "Two are better than one, because they have a good return for their labor: If either of them falls down, one can help the other up. But pity anyone who falls and has no one to help them up" (Ecclesiastes 4:9–10).

Early in our marriage, Karen and I started taking long walks together. We continued after our family came along, sometimes just to get a few quiet moments away from the chaos of a house full of three rambunctious kids. It was a good way for us to get some exercise, reconnect, and discuss the events of the day. When we lived in northern Virginia and served in Congress, we learned that my brother's wife, Denise, a Marine Corps spouse, was planning to do the Marine Corps Marathon (again). I had run in the 500 Festival Mini Marathons, 13.1 miles, back in Indianapolis a few times, but I had never considered running a full marathon. Inspired by our sister-in-law's example, we decided to do it.

Our goal was to alternate running and walking the 26.2 miles, but we knew we would still have to train to finish in the allotted time. So Karen and I trained together, putting in several miles in the early-morning hours before the kids were awake. We slowly built up to the pace and distance we needed to do the full marathon in under six hours. When the time came for the annual run, in late October 2009, we felt ready. Up before the sun rose, we were at the starting line near the Marine Corps Memorial, just across the Potomac River from Washington, DC. We milled around with thousands of other runners preparing to start the iconic race. We weren't on par with the marines preparing to complete the entire event at a running pace, but we had a goal. There is a time constraint that essentially determines whether someone finishes at all. Contestants must get to the Fourteenth Street Bridge at the twentieth mile[1] by 1:15 p.m. to be able to keep going and try to make it to the end.[2] If they don't reach the bridge by then, a bus picks them up and takes them to the finish line. This is called "beating the bridge," and we were determined to do it. We knew that if we "beat the bridge," we would finish.

The early miles of the race were easy. The air was cool, and as the sun came up, we both felt almost carried along by the throng of runners around us and the well-wishers lining the streets. Crossing the Potomac into Maryland, we wound our way through neighborhoods, even passing by the Vice President's Residence, never imagining that we would someday call it home. Early into the race, Karen started developing blisters on her feet. It was painful, but she's tough as nails, so she barely complained.

Around eighteen miles, we were halfway down the National Mall, passing the Smithsonian Institution's historic redbrick castle, when I started to notice that she was slowing down. The weird thing was that I felt great. It was as though my body was floating above the pavement and the people cheering me on were driving me to go faster and harder. I later understood that that was because of the rush of endorphins coursing through my body, the famous "runner's high." I felt as though I could sprint the next eight miles and finish in record time.

Karen could tell how I felt and saw that I could be going much faster. So she told me to go ahead and she would catch up with me later. With a nod, I surged forward into the crowd of runners. I felt a rush of adrenaline as I overtook runners I'd been trailing for the entire race, but then I caught myself. Karen and I had trained side by side, and I knew we needed to do the entire course together—whether or not we finished. I dialed down my speed and walked until she caught up with me in the crowd.

"What are you doing?" she asked as she came up on me.

"We trained together so we could run this race together," I said.

With a gentle smile, she nodded, and off we went.

A few miles later, we "beat the bridge" with less than ten minutes to spare. And after around six more miles, we crossed the finish line. Karen had blisters covering her feet, but she made it. And we did it together.

In that moment, I learned an important lesson: working toward a goal with someone you care about is more meaningful than doing it alone. And if you train together, you must cross the finish line together—even if you don't make it across at all.

Our campaigns for Congress, governor, vice president, and president were all races Karen and I ran together. I wasn't interested in trying to attain elected office without my family, without my wife. If Karen hadn't been on board, we wouldn't have done any of them. And through it all, we have held hands and celebrated victory, and we have held hands in the aftermath of defeat. The common thread that runs through these experiences is that we trained for and ran the races together, side by side.

Whatever race you're called to run, grab the hand of the one you love. Train together, and run the race together.

And whether you accomplish great things or share an effort that comes up short of your goal, when you cross that finish line, you will know that by God's grace, you got there together.

38

Take the Swing Set with You

The boundary lines have fallen for me in pleasant places.

—PSALM 16:6

In 1995, we finished building our dream home—our "home for tomorrow"—on the south side of Indianapolis.

At the time, our kids were young: two, three, and four years old. Since these are the ages when kids are meant to run wild, we knew we had to get our backyard into order. A fence separated the backyard from a large, open field of untouched land. Karen began by planting three trees at the back of the house, one for each kid. We seeded the lawn and planted flowers and shrubs along the front of the house and evergreens along the driveway. The yard was almost perfect, but the grassy expanse seemed to have too much space and was missing something. It needed the swing set we had had at our previous house.

So we had to bring it.

The kids were ecstatic about the prospect of having their miniature playground in the new backyard. It had two blue swings, a yellow slide, and a roofed fort in the middle that held it all together. The day it was delivered, they gathered on the porch and watched in awe as the moving truck arrived and settled it into the ground. Our kids enjoyed years of play on that swing set.

When we won a congressional election five years later, our children were still young, and we knew that moving to Washington, DC, would be a big change for them. They would be leaving their friends, school, and extended family to go to a new home in a new city where they didn't know anyone. We tried to make the transition as easy as possible for them, so when it came time to pack up our belongings and drive to Washington, we decided the swing set had to come with us. We knew it would be good for the kids to have something familiar from home, and Karen and I felt we couldn't part with it.

The large, weathered structure was made with sturdy two-by-fours. The blue plastic swings were perfect for long summer evenings when the sun didn't set until past the kids' bedtimes. The yellow slide had been a part of many a make-believe adventure, and sliding down it into a pile of freshly fallen leaves in the autumn months never failed to delight our kids. We made arrangements for the movers to load and haul the swing set all the way to our nation's capital.

We rented a home when we first arrived in Washington, but after a disagreement with the new landlord (who raised our rent and told us to get rid of our dog), we had to find somewhere else to live. It was a stressful situation, but God provided. Karen spent several days driving around northern Virginia looking for a rental home before she spotted a "for rent" sign in front of a house on Military Road, a busy street in Arlington, Virginia. She drove up the long driveway to find the landlord, and he agreed to rent it to us on the spot. We were out of the other home and moved into the new one within a week—with the swing set in tow.

During those early years in Congress, I would often say that we had a small home in Indiana and a smaller home in Washington, DC. After our first reelection, we started to look for a longer-term living situation. We wanted to buy a home in the suburban district where Karen wanted the kids to attend public high school. They wouldn't be going there for a few years, but we preferred to be settled in the county ahead of time. The prices of the homes in the area made it almost unfeasible for us to buy, but Karen found a 2,100-square-foot, two-story house while I was away on official business in Indiana for a few days. It was a redbrick home with green shutters on the windows and a spot for a flagpole on the doorframe. The house was up on a small rise and had an iron railing leading up the concrete steps to the front door.

When Karen called me, she told me we needed to make an offer immediately, and I told her to go for it, even though I hadn't seen it in person. Our offer was accepted, and in a few months' time, we moved into the place, moving out of our rental and hauling the swing set with us one more time.

For almost another decade, it graced our lawn. Karen landscaped around it. It brought joy to our children, their friends, and younger kids who visited our home. It was always there—stable, reliable, and a part of our story. It completed our backyard.

When we were getting ready to move home to Indiana to run for governor, we thought about taking the swing set with us like we had so many times. The wooden boards were getting worn down, the nails were rusting, and our kids had long since left the happy days on the slide and swings in the past. Karen and I decided that it was time to let the swing set go. We left it at the Arlington home we had purchased for the kids' high school years, satisfied to know that the next family would be able to enjoy it as much as our children had. Driving away from the house one last time in the U-Haul truck we had rented for the move home, I glanced over the back fence for one more look at our old swing set with a tear in my eye.

Many years and miles later, following the 2020 election, it was time for us to move home to Indiana again. We needed to find a place to live and wanted to get a house that could fit our three children and their families as they grew. After months of searching, Karen found the perfect spot. With five acres and a pond, the house sits on a small lane just north of Indianapolis. In summer, the leaves on the trees surrounding the house are green and lush. During the springtime, the birds are out in force, bringing their new families to see the blooming flowers in Karen's window boxes. During the winter, the pond freezes over and icicles hang from the trees surrounding it, acting as their own holiday decorations. The home is a blessing, and the peace it provides us is beyond compare, but after we moved in, it wasn't long until we realized it was incomplete. It needed a swing set.

We had only one grandchild when we moved in, so we decided we would wait to get a swing set until there were three in the family. No pressure. A little over a year later, our daughter and daughter-in-law each told us she was pregnant. In less than two years' time, we would welcome three beautiful granddaughters to our family. A few weeks later, there was a new swing set in the backyard, complete with swings for various ages, a slide, a child-sized rock wall, and a picnic table underneath, ready for a tea party.

The swing set our children had during those early years wasn't just a fun place for them to play; it was a consistent piece of their life. Taking it with us when we moved meant that there would be something dependable for them in each new home. It made the transitions a little less daunting, and we didn't leave it behind until we were ready to let it go. It doesn't have to be a swing set that travels with you, but holding on to the items that bring joy and a sense of continuity to your household can be a way to ease family members into the upheavals that invariably come.

Walking in from getting the newspaper in the morning, I often think of all the places we've called home and reflect on the verses "Lord, you alone are my portion and my cup; you make my lot secure. The boundary lines have fallen for me in pleasant places; surely I have a delightful inheritance" (Psalm 16:5–6). Over thirty years and eighteen moves, God has been good to our family, and we have strived every day to hold on to one another and to what matters.

When change comes in your life, hold on to the familiar, hold on to your family, and take the swing set with you.

39

Follow Your Instinct to Serve

*Each of you should use whatever gift you have received
to serve others.*

—1 PETER 4:10

When I was getting ready to graduate from high school, I grabbed a pamphlet for the United States Marine Corps at a career fair. The idea of serving my country after high school was appealing to me, and I thought it was a good plan. I brought it to my parents and thought my dad, who had served in the United States Army, would be supportive. To my surprise, he wasn't excited at all. I sat in the car with him outside our house on Hunter Place in Columbus, Indiana, and tried to convince him. He sternly informed me that he didn't want me to do it.

"You're going to college," he said. "Then you can go be a marine. But you're going to college."

He told me that if something had been going on overseas, things would be different. In that case, he would be in favor of me joining the military. But in 1977, the Vietnam War was over and the global War on Terror wouldn't begin for several decades.

As the first person in his family to receive a college degree, my father had always extolled the virtue of education. But honestly, I was shocked by his reaction. My dad had served in combat in the Korean War and come home with medals that had gone into a drawer, never to be spoken of again. Whenever people said he was a hero, he would always answer that the real heroes were the guys who hadn't come home. My mother once told me that he had woken up in a cold sweat from nightmares every night for the first ten years of their marriage because of what he had experienced in the war.

Like many who have seen combat, my dad was proud of his service, but he bore the invisible scars of war quietly and had no illusion about the sacrifices that come with serving in uniform. It would be years later, after I became a father, that I better understood my father's attitude that at seventeen years old remained a mystery.

I had little choice but to follow his advice and agreed to go to college.

When I graduated from Hanover College in 1981, there were a few years when I wasn't sure what I was going to do. I worked at my alma mater in the admissions department. I studied for the LSAT and applied to law schools. During those years, I could have joined the military, but for some reason, I never got back to it.

When I am asked about regrets of mine, several come to mind; never serving in uniform is one of them. I often tell young people today that if they have a desire to serve their country in politics and public life, there is no better training ground than the military. There are many ways in which to serve your country in the military, from the national guard to active duty to Reserve Officers' Training Corps (ROTC). Finding a way to do this, in whatever way it fits your life at the time, can be monumentally beneficial and educational. To these young people, I say: learn what it means to sacrifice for your country, and *then* go into the public arena.

In my roles as a congressman, governor, and vice president, I often met with and traveled to see members of our armed forces. I never failed to be amazed by the men and women who serve our country in uniform. They are from the rest of us, but they are the best of us. It's worth noting that the Bible records[1] that one of the only times Jesus was "amazed" was in a conversation with a centurion,[2] meaning a Roman soldier.

From all my time among America's finest, I wish I had recognized that initial calling to serve my country. It wouldn't have changed the trajectory of my career or broken my pace, and I regret that I didn't follow my first instinct, which was an instinct to serve. I'll always wish I had.

As a young man, I never understood why my father had discouraged me from entering military service. In fact, it wasn't until I had a son and a son-in-law in the military that I began to understand. My son was drawn to military service from a young age and is now a fighter pilot in the Marine Corps, and my daughter married a naval aviator from a great navy family. I've watched as they both deployed overseas, leaving their families for months on end, and I better understand the sacrifices that our service members and their families face. Additionally, in my years of public service, I've spent time with soldiers wounded in combat and poignant moments with families grieving an unimaginable loss. My dad saw things in combat in Korea that I hope and pray my son and son-in-law never see but I know that they and their families are prepared to see. The debt we owe to our service members and their families, especially those who "gave the last full measure of devotion,"[3] should inspire the gratitude and patriotism of every American.

There are many ways to serve. You can serve your state and nation through voluntary associations, your faith community, or myriad forms of government service. Service to others is always honorable. Though my life would eventually carry me into another career of service, I still regret that I didn't answer the call I had in my heart as a young man. So whatever form it may take, follow your instinct to serve.

40

Give Your Family Sunday

*Six days you shall labor and do all your work, but the
seventh day is a sabbath to the Lord your God. On it
you shall not do any work.*

—EXODUS 20:9-10

During the closing days of our second congressional campaign in 1990, I had an unfortunate encounter with a reporter. Though it was unwise at the time, it was a lesson to me in
the importance of rest.

Toward the end of the campaign, Karen and I were told
that we could use some campaign funds to pay a portion of our
mortgage and other personal expenses. At the time, that was
perfectly legal, and we had gone into some debt over the election season. Nevertheless, the press and my opponent seized on
the practice when we filed our campaign reports, putting it in
the worst possible light.

When a reporter called to ask me about it, I lost my tem-
per. My reaction ended up being half of the story, making a bad
story even worse. The reporter had called me on a Monday after
we had spent the previous Sunday on the campaign trail. I was

exhausted and hadn't given myself time to mentally decompress from the week.

We ended up losing that election, but we lost more than a congressional race; we lost sight of our values. We didn't advance the conservative cause in a way that reflected our Christian faith. My conversation with that reporter was one of many situations that made us realize we would need to do things differently if we ever entered politics again.

As a result, when we were heading back into the political arena to run for Congress a third time, we came up with several practical habits to guide us. Though it was a decade later, we knew it would be easy to run the same way we had in the past. Instead, we decided to run the race on a foundation of experience and timeless wisdom. We wanted to run a campaign that we would be proud of and would put our family first.

Most important, Karen and I agreed that we would not campaign on Sundays. The Bible is clear about the need for us to rest on the Sabbath, saying "And on the seventh day God finished his work that he had done, and he rested on the seventh day from all his work that he had done. So God blessed the seventh day and made it holy, because on it God rested from all his work that he had done in creation" (Genesis 2:2–3). We need to be productive to be fulfilled, but we also need to end our work. It's important to take a break. This doesn't apply only to people who are in the workforce. Homemakers and primary caregivers of a household also need rest, even and especially when it seems they have no time to relax.

Karen and I wanted to honor God with our campaign choices, and keeping the Sabbath was one way we could do it. It wasn't easy, as there are often picnics and events on the weekends during an election cycle, as well as numerous invitations to attend church services. But it was a promise we made, and we intended to keep it.

For us, Sunday was the anchor in our week, and we guarded it jealously. Even during my days in Congress, on weekends when I would travel to Indiana, I always made it a point to try to be home for church on Sunday. That often meant catching an inconvenient flight or missing out on a function in my home state, but it always made the week better. I learned that my wife and children could endure the separation of a very hectic weekly work schedule if they knew we reserved Sundays for family. Even when I was on the road during the week, or spent late nights on Capitol Hill, they could depend on Sunday and the fact that Dad would be home. It was a consistency, and by honoring it, I honored them.

Karen and I wanted our children to know that Sundays were a time when they could catch up with us. They always knew that no matter how busy the week was or how scattered our family may have seemed with our parallel schedules that often didn't overlap, on Sundays, we would be together. Because of that, we didn't encourage our kids to participate in travel sports that would require them to be on the road on Sunday mornings. We didn't have anything against sports, and all of our kids were active in extracurricular activities, but we wanted Sundays to be special.

Sunday mornings in the Pence home were often filled with the smell of omelets cooking on the stove. After church, we went home and changed into comfortable clothes. If it was a sunny spring or summer day in northern Virginia, we grilled chicken or burgers in the backyard. During the fall, football was always on television. In the winter, the living room was never without a fire in the fireplace. We all read books, the kids worked on homework, and everyone tried to take a nap in the afternoon. Those were times of deep rest for our family.

Karen and I still do our best to avoid campaigning or working on Sundays, but I know firsthand how hard it is to maintain this habit. While I was serving as vice president, by late afternoon on Sundays, work would demand my attention. During that time, I compromised by setting aside the mornings for church and the early afternoons for family and rest before putting in a few hours of work.

These days, Sundays often involve calls from our children, who are all married with families of their own. It gives me joy to hear that most Sundays our adult children are taking it easy, and I can often hear a grandchild in the background.

A day of rest doesn't have to look the same for everyone, and in the Jewish faith, it falls on Friday night and lasts through Saturday. The most important thing is that taking a day off for your family provides the recuperation and connection that you all need. Rest provides a sense of clarity, and spending it with loved ones gives us perspective in a world where everything else seems to be vying for our attention. Putting aside your work, closing your laptop, and silencing your phone to mentally and physically rest at the end of the week is not only good for you, it creates a day on which your family will rely.

Rest from your labor, and give your family Sunday.

41

Take Your Spouse There

Husbands, love your wives.

—EPHESIANS 5:25

O utside my relationship with God, my marriage is the foundation of my life. When Karen and I were first married, it was easy to make time for each other. We would take in dinner and a movie, walk to a nearby canal to feed the ducks, or just sit on our front porch swing talking about our day. The time we spent together early on helped us to remember to prioritize each other as life became more crowded.

As a child, Karen always wanted to go to Disney World. I have fond memories of Pence family vacations to Disneyland in California and a few trips to Disney World in Florida as a young man, but her family had never been able to make it to either location. We both used to talk about how, when our family came along, we would take our own children to "the happiest place on Earth."

But after we got married, we experienced years of unexplained infertility, and the period of waiting was unrelenting. We, like so many other couples, went through a seemingly unending cycle of hope and disappointment. After five years, we weren't sure if we would ever have children of our own or live the dream that we could someday walk our kids through the turnstiles of the Magic Kingdom. So instead of delaying Karen's childhood dream any longer, we decided to go ourselves.

Arriving at Disney World in Orlando, Florida, in the summer of 1988, as two grown adults, we thought we might look a little out of place, but we were thrilled to be there. We spent the entire day in the parks, walking miles under the hot Florida sun to see every sight Karen had grown up imagining. She was a kid again.

We ate European food in EPCOT and explored the Magic Kingdom. Karen took pictures with the different characters, and I can still see her amazing smile beaming next to Mickey Mouse. It was a special time. Though we trusted God and prayed that He would bring us a family one day, we didn't want life to pass us by while we waited. Going to Disney World with Karen is one of my favorite memories from my "life before kids."

Ten years and three kids later, we made it back to Disney. It was the spring of 2000, and we had finally won the Republican primary in the second district of Indiana against five worthy opponents. It was a hard-fought campaign, and our kids had spent the entire year going to parades and picnics. We wanted to celebrate their hard work with a family vacation.

Karen and I had enjoyed our time at the theme park years before, but when we arrived at the entrance of the Magic Kingdom and other tourists swarmed around us, something happened that I will never forget.

As we made our way through the turnstiles and our kids rushed into the park, hoping to catch a glimpse of Cinderella's Castle, I looked over at my wife. Michael, Charlotte, and Audrey were eight, seven, and six years old at the time, and they were ready for the day with their snack-filled fanny packs and Mickey Mouse ear hats. But their mother took a moment to stand amid the crowd, the pounding Disney music, and the sights. Pushing her sunglasses up onto her head, I saw tears streaming down her face. And I knew why.

I grabbed her hand, and she squeezed mine back. "I just never thought I would get this moment," she said. But she didn't have to explain. I wiped away a few tears myself. After years of heartache, deep longing, and prayer, we had made it. God had fulfilled our dream of having children, and the dream of serving in our nation's capital was unfolding before our eyes. We were proud of our team and felt humbled that Hoosiers had trusted us with a chance to run in the fall election. But after years of personal and professional disappointment, that success was nothing compared to winning that moment with our entire family, now complete with our children beside us. It was one of the happiest moments of my life.

The joy of seeing our children at Disney World was inexpressible, but I'm glad that Karen and I didn't wait until we had kids to go there. I'm grateful that we relished our life even when we wanted more out of it.

Karen and I would go on to travel the world together during our time serving in the House of Representatives, the Indiana Statehouse, and the White House. And although we were blessed with rich memories, we tried to remember that those official trips were not the same as family vacations. Just as we had had to prioritize travel together even when we didn't have children, we had to be sure to make time for each other in the hectic schedule of politics. That was especially true when I was vice president, when changes in the schedule can come at a moment's notice.

After taking years of French in grade school and high school, Karen spoke the language almost fluently and has always adored French culture. For our twentieth wedding anniversary, we fulfilled a lifelong dream of hers by visiting Paris, the City of Light. We walked the narrow cobblestone streets and visited art museums to see the creations she had spent decades studying. Our likenesses were captured in a charcoal drawing in Montmartre, we walked beside the Seine, and we enjoyed coffee and *chocolat* in the local cafés. But the high point was traveling to the home of one of her favorite Impressionist artists, Claude Monet. We took the train to Giverny, just outside Paris, and toured the artist's famous pink house and adjacent garden. I watched Karen walk, almost transfixed, across the Japanese bridge that Monet had captured in his paintings. The scenery had inspired Monet to paint the famous water lilies, artworks she had spent her career teaching to her students. The trip was more than a sightseeing vacation; it was an affirmation of Karen's passions and her immense talents as a teacher and an artist.

You don't have to travel to Europe to fulfill your spouse's dreams; sometimes it just takes a drive to the Sunshine State. Of course, taking time for a vacation isn't always easy. And it certainly wasn't always possible for us to get away. But uplifting your spouse's dreams is what matters, and this can be done in lots of ways: over a dinner date, during front porch conversations, or on long car rides. The activity doesn't have to be expensive; your spouse just needs to know that you see and support his or her ambitions.

So never forget, as you pursue your dreams, to take time to find out the faraway places and the quiet dreams of the one you love. And the first chance you get, by all means, take her there.

42

Learn from Falling Short

For we all stumble in many ways. And if anyone does
not stumble in what he says, he is a perfect man.

—JAMES 3:2

In 2013, a few weeks after I had been sworn in as governor of
Indiana, I was set to give a speech outlining my vision for the
upcoming session of the Indiana state legislature. It was my first
year in office; the Indiana General Assembly was already going
full speed ahead, and I was trying to get my administration moving forward on the agenda I had campaigned on and been elected
to advance. Time was of the essence. I wanted to deliver for the
people of Indiana and make a good first impression right out of
the gate.

I was scheduled to give the speech at a business event in
Fort Wayne in the northeast corner of the state. As I left the
Statehouse midafternoon to head to the airport, my cell phone
rang. It was Karen, calling to tell me that she had been experiencing pain in her abdomen and was heading to the hospital.

Early in the day, she had started to feel ill at her office. She
had lain down on the couch and taken antacids to ease her
stomach pain but had eventually told her security detail, a state

trooper named Jimmy Cruse, that she needed to go home. On the way to the Governor's Residence, the pain got worse, and she told him she needed to go to the hospital instead. Jimmy turned on the car's police lights and rushed her to the emergency room.

Once she arrived, doctors conducted tests to see if she was having a heart attack, which thankfully came back negative. She called to let me know the results, that she was stable and in the care of physicians. By that time, I was getting ready to board my plane. There were around a thousand people waiting to hear me speak, and I was anxious at the thought of canceling. I felt compelled to do the speech to prove my commitment to my new job. I was afraid that people wouldn't understand a last-minute cancellation. Ultimately, I let my fear of how people might react cloud my judgment.

Over the phone, Karen told me that the doctors were going to do an ultrasound of her gallbladder to see if it was the cause of her pain. Predictably, my stoic wife said that I should go to the event, that it was nothing serious and they would do surgery the following day if her gallbladder needed to be removed. I ended the call by asking her to call Audrey, since the hospital was near our daughter's school. After her mother had reached her, to her credit, Audrey did what I should have done: she immediately left school to sit with her mom and took her home from the hospital once she was discharged.

I went to the speech. My address and agenda were well received, but it didn't matter. Flying home that night, all I could think about was the poor choice I had made.

I chose my work instead of my wife that day, and I have regretted it ever since. I am married to a gracious woman and she forgave me, but I am not sure I have ever forgiven myself. I was home that night and by her side for the rest of her treatment, surgery, and recovery. But I should have dropped everything and immediately gone to the hospital. I didn't give her what she deserved in that moment, and I also didn't give Hoosiers enough credit. The people of Indiana have strong hearts, they look after their neighbors, and they love their families. I have no doubt that the good people of Fort Wayne would have understood why I needed to cancel my speech. Instead, I let fear get the best of me. I've tried to do better ever since.

A decade later, faced with a similar choice, I made a different decision. In February 2023, on the day my daughter Charlotte was in labor with her first child, I was scheduled for a full day in South Carolina. There was attention on the prospect of my running for president, so it was a busy time. We had events lined up back-to-back, and people had been putting the schedule together for weeks. But when we heard that Charlotte was heading to the hospital, I canceled everything. As I was informed by my previous failure, it was a much easier choice to make that time around. Karen and I got onto a plane as soon as we could to meet our granddaughter.

After we saw Charlotte and her family, I called a chief of police in South Carolina who had organized many of the events to apologize. He told me there was no need. He said that people in the Palmetto State think highly of me because of my family values, and when they had heard why I had postponed the trip, they hadn't been surprised. It was what they expected me to do. By God's grace, that time I made the right decision. You've got to love South Carolina.

The Bible says that "we all stumble in many ways" (James 3:2). To me, this is a great comfort. It means that we can—and will—make mistakes. The real lesson I learned from those two experiences was how to admit my failure and to commit to making a different decision in the future. You won't always live up to the values you hold, but recognizing when you fall short is the only way to grow.

When you fall short, own it and learn from it. And have faith that people will understand—and respect—you when you make a decision that aligns with your values.

43

Use Your Authority to Put Your Family First

Be shepherds of God's flock that is under your care, watching over them—not because you must, but because you are willing.

—1 PETER 5:2

O ur son, Michael, and his fiancée, Sarah, were married in a small ceremony at the Indiana Governor's Residence on December 28, 2016. They wanted to be married soon after their engagement and live together near Michael's base, Naval Air Station Meridian, in Meridian, Mississippi. Since Michael is in the military, they also set a date, as many military couples do, for a large wedding ceremony and reception in Brown County, Indiana, in October of the following year.

I was sworn in as vice president in January 2017, and the Secret Service protection—complete with a lengthy motorcade of black SUVs, motorcycles, and medical personnel—traveled with me everywhere. I was familiar with having a security detail because of the state police who had been assigned to me when I was governor of Indiana, but the level of protection escalated monumentally once I became vice president and the Secret Service took over. Sometimes we didn't even know all of the moving parts that kept us safe. It was humbling to be surrounded by men and women who put their lives on the line for my family and me—not because of who we were but because of the position we held.

When October arrived, the travel entourage was scheduled to arrive in Brown County a few days before Michael's wedding. The logistics had already proven to be a bit of a headache, but the staff at the Abe Martin Lodge in Brown County State Park were extremely accommodating.

For years, Brown County State Park has been a safe haven for our family. It is home to the Aynes House, a cabin used as a retreat for the Indiana governor and family. Karen had raised private funding to renovate the hundred-year-old cabin during our time in the Statehouse. We had used it countless times during my time as governor, and Governor Eric Holcomb and his wife, Janet, were kind enough to let us use it during our time at the White House, as well. It was a true gift. The staff there never failed to make it feel like home when we didn't have a place of our own.

Time and again, we drove the winding roads through the wooded state park up to the small log cabin. Once on the grounds, I could look to the right and see my favorite view in the state of Indiana. The tops of trees stretch for miles, and in the fall, the colors of the changing leaves look like a multicolored quilt. A great sense of peace washed over me anytime I gazed across the landscape. I read on the front porch and sat by the fire with my family as we deliberated over major decisions. I will always be grateful for the clarity and insight I gained at Aynes House.

Air Force Two landed at the regional airport in Columbus,

Indiana, a few days before Michael's wedding, transporting our-selves, the groom, and other necessary items for the wedding festivities. We disembarked on the metal stairs brought up to the side of the plane, and Michael went to the underbelly of the plane to grab his gear. He asked members of my staff and the Secret Service agents if they could open the cargo hold so he could take his belongings to one of the cabins and get ready for the rehearsal dinner, which was only a few hours away.

The agents informed him of their policy not to unload any-thing until the vice president and second lady left the area. As the principal "protectees," we had to be in the cars and they would have to wait until the motorcade had departed before they were allowed to get anything out of the plane. I made my way down to the tarmac and noticed Michael standing nearby without any of his bags. Michael understood rank, so he wasn't going to press the issue, but he did let me know they couldn't open the plane until I was gone.

I turned to the lead agent and said, "Open the plane."

"Yes, sir," he replied, and they got to work.

Michael was amused by the situation but not surprised. He understood chain of command. In the military and law enforce-ment, it's standard to follow procedure, but if a person with a higher level of authority gives a different directive, that takes precedence.

I learned the same thing during my time as governor and vice president. The members of my security detail were trained to adhere to certain standards, but they were always allowed to change course if I said so. It gave me the opportunity to put my family first in a new way—by using the authority I had been granted to intervene in situations such as this one.

The Bible speaks about the concept of authority. When

Jesus encountered a centurion, which was a military officer in ancient times, the man told Jesus that his servant was paralyzed.

"Shall I come and heal him?" Jesus asked.

"Lord, I do not deserve to have you come under my roof. But just say the word, and my servant will be healed. For I myself am a man under authority, with soldiers under me. I tell this one, 'Go,' and he goes; and that one, 'Come,' and he comes. I say to my servant, 'Do this,' and he does it," the centurion responded.

The military leader understood the concept of authority. He had faith that if Jesus wanted something to be done, He had only to speak and it would happen. The centurion's servant was "healed at that moment" (Matthew 8:7–13).

In your life, your level of authority might vary. It certainly has in mine. There may be times your family will be the primary place where you have the authority to make decisions or take command of a situation. It may be in the workplace or in a volunteer environment. The idea of wielding power can be uncomfortable, but understanding the authority you have provides an opportunity to put your family first, particularly in situations where they otherwise might feel unimportant or undervalued.

Michael needed to know that I was going to do everything I could to support him on his wedding day, and that moment allowed me to show him that. Especially outside the home, it isn't always clear to family members that they are more important than whatever is going on at the time.

So when you have the chance, send the message that you will always put your family first.

44

Buy a Red Truck

A cheerful heart is good medicine.

—PROVERBS 17:22

Wherever life has taken the Pence family, we've gone there in a red truck. From the home we maintained in Indiana throughout my congressional years to the several homes we rented in Virginia, all the way to the governor's residence of Indiana, there was a consistent character: at every place the Pences called home, you could glance out the window and see a red truck parked outside.

I've graduated from law school, been a governor, and served in the White House. I've met with kings, prime ministers, and presidents all over the world, but I'm still the kid who grew up with a cornfield in my backyard. Having a truck throughout my political career—from Indiana to Washington and back again—reminded me who I was and where I came from.

I've ridden in motorcades and flown on Air Force Two and in helicopters and military aircraft, but on a Saturday morning, I want to be driving a truck with the sweet smell of fresh crops coming in through the open windows. There's nothing quite like driving your daughter to the local gas station to pick up doughnuts, a newspaper, and a few cups of coffee in a red truck. Charlotte and I used to get up and drive down 800 North to Thornton's gas station in Columbus, Indiana, before the other kids were awake. Those are still some of my favorite memories of the two of us.

After our first term in Congress, we purchased our first red truck for me to drive in Washington. It was an endearing little 1996 Chevy S-10 with no back seat but a jump seat wedged between the driver and passenger. The windows had to be rolled down with a crank, and to accelerate, you had to floor it.

We also bought a larger Chevy Silverado to remain in Indiana for the campaign. When I drove past rows of soybean fields and stalks of corn on a two-lane road in southern Indiana on my way to an event, it was easy to imagine that I was living out a country song. That truck went everywhere with us—hauling flyers, signs, candy to pass out at parades, and plastic bags with our slogan on them to give away at county fairs. It was known as the Big Red Truck, or BRT, as I liked to call it, and our first truck was dubbed the Little Red Truck, or LRT.

The LRT wasn't much use with its lack of space, and we had a better idea for it. On Charlotte's eighteenth birthday, we told her we wanted to show her something outside. When she walked out the front door of our home in northern Virginia, she saw it: the LRT parked on the street, all hers. We knew there was no one who would love driving the LRT through the streets of northern Virginia and Washington, DC, more than Charlotte, who had spent her youth looking forward to visiting Indiana so she could go for a spin in the BRT.

Running for governor of Indiana meant moving back to the Hoosier State. As we packed up our house in Arlington, Virginia, we deliberated over what to do with the LRT. She was on her last legs, and the logical choice would have been to sell her on the East Coast before we left, but we just couldn't bring ourselves to do it. With me driving our loaded U-Haul, Karen trailed behind, driving the Little Red Truck across the country to Indiana, and it broke down only twice on the way. The truck wouldn't leave the state again, and we drove her only short distances, but she made it back to where she belonged.

The BRT worked hard during our campaign for governor, and it became an emblem of the election. We drove it around the State on our "Big Red Truck Tour," meeting with voters and sharing our message of how we would make Indiana "a state that works."

When the time finally came for us to part ways with the Little Red Truck, Karen took it to a dealership. As she handed over the single metal key that had faithfully started the engine for years and watched as the workers drove the truck away, she shed a few tears. The LRT had been through a lot with us, and it had begun a tradition in our family.

The trucks became a rallying point and a small part of our identity. Michael and Charlotte's families, serving in our armed forces on the other side of the country, now both have red trucks of their own. I like to think that wherever they go in life, their trucks will remind them of the cornfields of Indiana and driving at night down a two-lane country road with countless stars overhead. I also hope that the practicality of a truck reminds them of other values we share—of lending a neighbor a hand, of the satisfaction of hard work, and of making time to create traditions with their children.

After the 2020 election, we moved back home to Indiana. Since Karen and I hadn't driven ourselves during the four years we had had Secret Service protection, we had to buy a couple cars right away. The one I picked out was fine and got the job done, but my son wasn't impressed. When he was packing up after Christmas with us that first year, he told me with a wry smile, "Dad, if you don't have a red truck by Christmas next year, I'm not coming home."

There's nothing I love more than to please my children, so the red Ford Ranger he requested is in my garage.

It doesn't have to be a red truck that your family shares. It can be anything that serves as a reminder of home and values that you prize. The Bible tells us that if we "train up a child in the way he should go . . . he will not depart from it" (Proverbs 22:6). Look for things that will remind you and your family where you come from, and you'll see more clearly where you can go.

And when in doubt, buy the red truck.

45

When You're Being Honored, Honor Your Family

Who am I, Sovereign Lord, and what is my family, that you have brought me this far?

—2 SAMUEL 7:18

When House Majority Leader Dick Armey of Texas retired, an official portrait of him was hung in the halls of the Capitol building. I had admired Armey from afar for many years; he was a household name among conservatives and well known by Republicans around the country.

One day, I remember walking past the portrait and noticing a striking detail: the painting was meant to honor his service in public life, but it included a framed photo on his desk of his wife, Susan, with almost as much detail as his own likeness. I appreciated the fact that he had included a picture of his spouse in a representation that served as a testament to his career. When people saw the portrait and remembered him, they would remember her, too.

Years later, I found myself in a similar position. Portraits of Indiana governors hang in the lobby of the governor's office in the Statehouse. During my first year as vice president, the time came for my official Indiana governor portrait to be painted. After narrowing it down to three finalists, I finally decided on an artist from the Hoosier State, Mark Dillman. Mark told me that he had supported me since our very first campaign. Since the portrait would hang in the Indiana Statehouse for years to come, I figured it was a good idea to choose someone to paint it who actually liked me.

Mark and his wife, Lynn, traveled to the Vice President's Residence in Washington, DC, for an afternoon to snap some photographs. I had to decide on the specifics—what I wanted to wear and if any props should be included. During the several decades I have served in politics, I've seen a lot of portraits. But the memory of Armey's tribute stuck out. Like him, I wanted to recognize all that had led to my serving my state as governor. If you happen to walk the marble halls of the Indiana Statehouse and find the portrait hanging there, you will see a few details that are the heart of the painting. In fact, they are the real reason why that portrait is hanging there at all.

In the portrait, there are three books stacked on the desk behind me, which represent my dad's law books from the one semester of law school he attended. He gave them to me when I graduated from the Indiana University Robert H. McKinney School of Law in 1986. I continued the tradition and presented them to my daughter Audrey when she graduated from Yale Law School more than three decades later. She was touched to receive them, but she insisted that I keep one since they were a gift from my own father. Dad went to law school for one semester before he met my mother and left to earn a living. We all stand on the shoulders of those who went before, and everything I am I owe to the sacrifices, the successes, and the efforts of my dad, Ed Pence, and my wonderful mother, Nancy Pence-Fritsch. Those books are part of my story.

I also wanted to be sure that the painting included the American flag and the state flag of Indiana, as well as a reproduction of the Bible that sat on my congressional desk in Washington, DC, in the Indiana Statehouse, and eventually in the White House. When I took the oath of office to become governor of Indiana, that very Bible was opened to a verse that is really a prayer: "Give your servant a discerning heart to govern your people and to distinguish between right and wrong. For who is able to govern this great people of yours?" (1 Kings 3:9). It felt fitting to include my Bible in the portrait since it had guided me through so many days serving in the governor's office.

To the left on the desk is a photo of my family. The framed picture of the five of us was on my credenza throughout my time in public life. It, too, was displayed when I was a congressman, when I was a governor, and after I made it to the West Wing of the White House. The highest titles I will ever hold are husband and dad, so I wanted to be sure that Michael, Charlotte, Audrey, and Karen were all in the portrait, too. My family is the clearest evidence of God's grace and faithfulness. Any honor paid to me must include them.

The artist, Mark Dillman, told me that the painting turned out to be one of his best pieces of work, and considering what he had to work with, I would have to agree. It not only summarizes my time in public life and the people who got me there but also includes another special, almost hidden tribute.

When people look at the painting, the person I really want them to see is not me but rather someone who is just out of frame, who has been the rock I have needed time and time again. That person is my wonderful wife, Karen. I wore a tie that she designed while she was first lady of Indiana and made sure my wedding ring was visible. But there's another tribute to her included in the portrait that was entirely unintentional.

During the photo session for the portrait, I was uncomfortable and visibly stiff in the many photos Mark and Lynn took. Mark told me to lean back and fold my arms, but the position was unnatural and I felt awkward. My mind wasn't at ease, either. I couldn't stop thinking about whatever battles our administration was fighting that day. I also knew that the portrait would be the representation of me in my home state for years to come, and I could feel my body physically unable to relax. After about an hour of picture taking, I was exhausted, but hardly any of the photos were usable. My smile was awkward and flat.

When we received the photos from Mark, my family and I looked through them to select the one we wanted him to use. There was only one where I looked at ease. It was also the only one where I was glancing off to the side, my eyes focused on something just out of view. Hands down, everyone agreed it was the best picture and we had to use it, but then I remembered why it was better.

During the photo shoot, Karen had walked down the stairs at the Vice President's Residence to check on me. She could probably sense that things were not going well. As she peeked around the corner, I looked away from the camera and smiled at her. Just then, Lynn, Mark's wife, took the picture. In the portrait to this day, I am looking away and smiling because I am looking at my wife.

The fact that Karen is the object of my gaze in the portrait is more than just a nice story. It exemplifies our life in politics. We did it all together, and the times I had the most peace were when she was by my side, when my focus was on her.

That portrait now graces the halls of the governor's office at the Indiana Statehouse. It will remain where our hearts will always be, where the moon shines bright upon the Wabash River in our Indiana home, as the famous song goes.[1] It is my prayer that schoolchildren passing by for decades will glance at it and, in one portrait, see honor paid to my parents, my family, my country, my state, and my wife. I also hope they notice the Bible sitting on my desk and know that everything my little family was able to do was because of God's faithfulness in our lives.

As King David asks the Lord, "Who am I, Sovereign Lord, and what is my family, that you have brought me this far?" (2 Samuel 7:18). Whatever your career or calling in life, seize the times when the limelight is shining on you and divert it to your family. Reflect the praise onto them, and make sure they are properly recognized for their contributions and sacrifices.

When you are being honored, honor your family.

46

Pass the Dad Test

*As a father has compassion on his children, so the Lord
has compassion on those who fear him.*

—PSALM 103:13

The 2020 presidential election would put our family through another transition, but the biggest change had nothing to do with politics.

The country had been through a difficult time while the Covid-19 pandemic spread throughout the world, shutting down travel, businesses, and schools. Though our administration had urged the public to stay home for a few weeks so that medical personnel could get the equipment they needed for the anticipated surge of the virus, Democratic governors had taken the opportunity to close schools and businesses, increasing people's reliance on government and government spending for months on end.

It was a hardship on American families and did little, if anything, to restrain the virus. Families lost loved ones, often unable to say goodbye because of quarantines. Countless family and community events were canceled or postponed, creating an even greater sense of isolation for millions of Americans. Our family was no different.

When the virus hit, our younger daughter, Audrey, and her fiancé, Dan Tomanelli, were in the final stages of planning a wedding in Kauai, Hawaii. Like so many couples around the world, they postponed the ceremony they had planned for May 2020. They rescheduled it for August, when it was widely believed that the coronavirus would no longer be a threat. But they were forced to delay it several more times when restrictions resurfaced.

By November 2020, Americans were growing tired of the lockdowns that had been forced onto them in cities and states across the country. It seemed as if the restrictions would never be lifted, and it was taking a toll on families. Since Audrey and Dan had already spent months waiting to get married and they weren't sure when they would ever be able to have a large celebration, Audrey came to Karen and me with an idea.

She called her mother a few weeks before election day. She wanted to know if it would be possible for her and Dan to get married on November 1, the Sunday before election day. Her siblings and grandparents would be in Washington for the election, and with a possible overseas military deployment coming up for Michael, she wanted to make every effort to have her brother at her wedding.

Anticipating her call and considering our breakneck pace campaigning across the country, my mind flooded with stress-ridden thoughts at the prospect of watching our youngest child being married—and hosting a wedding—a few days before the presidential election. But I paused and reminded myself about the principles by which I try to live.

When the call came in, I feigned ignorance as Audrey said, "Dad, we were thinking of going ahead and getting married on November 1, when everybody's in town."

After a long pause, I replied, "You know, that's two days before the election," to which she shyly replied, "Yeah."

And I just took a deep breath and said, "What a great idea!"

In the weeks leading up to the election, I was campaigning nonstop. Our team traveled less that year than in 2016 due to the pandemic, but I was still trying to visit as many states as I could in the final days. Audrey and her mom were busy coordinating wedding plans, finding a new dress for her to wear, and deciding where the couple would exchange their vows. Audrey even asked me to lead the ceremony and marry the two of them. It was one of the greatest honors I have ever been given—and also one of the hardest.

I warned her with a chuckle that even though it was a civil ceremony, if I was leading the service, I was going to "bring it" and talk about the importance of faith to our marriage and theirs. And she replied, "We want you to, Dad."

It was a rainy November day in Washington, but the sun came out long enough for us to take pictures outside the Vice President's Residence before we made our way downtown. Because of Covid-19 restrictions, our entire group wasn't allowed inside the courthouse, so we gathered on the street outside the building as the couple prepared to say their vows.

Audrey was glowing and beautiful. She wore a ruffled white dress, saving her formal wedding gown for the large celebration they still wanted to hold someday. Charlotte had done her makeup that morning, and Audrey's classic cropped hair framed her face. She held a small bouquet of calla lilies and white roses, beaming at Dan as I began the ceremony during a break in the weather. They said their vows and exchanged the rings that had been purchased before anyone had ever heard of the coronavirus.

I recited a verse that Karen and I had used in our wedding in June 1985. It's from Ecclesiastes and states that "A cord of three strands is not quickly broken." I reminded them that if they built their marriage on faith in God, they, too, would be a "cord of three strands." As I pronounced them husband and wife, the clouds broke overhead, and a vibrant sunset painted the sky in a blessing over the couple. It was glorious.

That evening, we all had dinner at a local restaurant. With toasts and prayers, we sent them off into their new life. Karen, Michael, Charlotte, and Sarah had decorated their gray Jeep Compass with streamers, bows, bells, and window paint that proclaimed, "COVID can't stop love!"

As the night wound down, we knew it was time to say goodbye. We huddled outside, blowing bubbles for them to run through, and Audrey, wearing a tan coat over her dress, ducked into the car. She turned around and made her fingers into the shape of a circle, a gesture our family has done for years as a prayer of safekeeping over departing family members. We did the same as we watched the gray Jeep drive away down the city street, the words "Just Married" proudly displayed on the back window.

There will be moments in your life when you will face a test that comes in the form of a request from your children. They won't necessarily be testing you on purpose. But when they ask you to do something, knowing that the easy answer would be "No," and you say "Yes," they will always remember it.

Panic may set in momentarily. Reasons to stick to the plan will be front of mind. Those valid concerns will try to force their way out of your mouth and into the conversation. I know what I'm talking about. This has happened to me more often than I care to admit. You think of all the ways that whatever they are asking you to do is inconvenient and near impossible. This is the time to pause and get a broader perspective. Try to think about what you will remember years from now, when everything is said and done.

When you say "Yes," you show your children that they matter more than anything else. So say "Yes" when you can, even if everything else is telling you to say "No." Pass the Dad test.

47

Get Away with Family

How good and pleasant it is when God's people live together in unity!

—PSALM 133:1

When I was governor of Indiana, I entered a time of unexpected testing. But the period of difficulty taught me an important lesson that I would rely on years later: when traveling through a deep valley, surround yourself with family.

In the spring of 2015, the Religious Freedom Restoration Act (RFRA) passed with overwhelming majorities in both the House and Senate of the Indiana General Assembly, and I signed it without hesitation. I have always supported the freedom of religion of every American of every faith. As it appeared that the Supreme Court would rule in favor of same-sex marriage, Indiana legislators—myself included—wanted to make sure that Hoosiers who believed in traditional marriage were still protected under the law.

As soon as I signed the bill, the progressive Left and their allies in the media descended upon Indiana. Leftist groups were positioned to criticize and boycott our state. It was one of the first battles between woke America and the American people.

Hoosiers were unfairly maligned and labeled as intolerant and bigoted, even though nothing could be further from the truth. I was defensive of the people of my state, who were being grossly misrepresented on the national stage. And I was being personally dragged through the mud, as well. Everyone on the left, on the right, and in the middle was busy counting me out of any future in politics.

Karen was visiting our girls in Europe, so I was alone in Indiana for much of the onslaught. Audrey was spending a semester in Istanbul, and Charlotte was studying abroad in England, so the three of them met up in Turkey for a vacation. Afterward, they headed to Greece to celebrate Easter as I dealt with the week's ordeal back in Indiana.

As the busy and emotionally exhausting week at the Statehouse was drawing to a close, so were the criticisms. With a moment to finally breathe, Karen suggested that I should travel to Greece to surprise Audrey. We told Charlotte so she could help with the logistics. On Friday afternoon, I left the Statehouse, avoiding the assembled state and national media. I dashed to my car in a rainstorm and headed to the airport. I boarded a plane to New York and landed in Athens the following day to be with my girls. Beneath the blue sky and striking Greek sunlight, I immediately felt better.

The Acropolis of Athens dates back to prehistoric times and rests atop a limestone hill looking over the city of Athens.[1] It has survived natural and man-made attacks for thousands of years. Karen and Charlotte had told me they would be there. As I arrived on the historic grounds, I spotted them, with Audrey leading a tour of the site with her mother and sister and explaining the history and significance of the ruins. Charlotte saw me approach and tried to maintain her composure. It was windy, so I walked up behind Audrey and asked, "Anybody need a sweatshirt?"

Audrey ignored me at first, thinking I was a vendor, but then was stunned and confused when she turned and saw me there. We all laughed and embraced in a big hug. The rest of the trip was just what I needed. I was exhausted and stressed by the response to RFRA, but I was filled with complete peace being with my family. Walking atop the Acropolis with my wife and daughters brought an unspeakable comfort to my heart.

Later that week, we had dinner at a restaurant where we could see the Parthenon brightly lit against the darkened night sky. We were awed to see the pillars on those heights that during thousands of years had stood the test of time. I took a moment to appreciate where I was and realized how renewed and refreshed I felt by being with my family.

Just as the birth of Michael had healed my heart after losing my dad so many years ago, simply seeing my girls brought a deep sense of calm. Our visit reminded me that my family would still be there even if my career was over.

Of course, I would go on to do much more in politics. But the vacation in Greece taught me the importance of grounding myself with my family after an intense professional time. I would draw on that wisdom five years later during the waning days of my service as vice president.

After the 2020 presidential election, our family spent the holidays in Vail, Colorado. The events leading up to that trip, and what would happen after it, made me grateful that God had granted us that time together as a family.

In December, I felt increasing pressure over my role in certifying the presidential election. When I was boarding Air Force Two to Vail, President Trump cryptically retweeted an article titled "Operation Pence Card," which suggested that I could alter the outcome of the election when Congress gathered on January 6, 2021. Although I had told the president my position several times and was certain that the Constitution did not give me any such power, his retweet gave even greater attention to the theory.

Showing the tweet to Karen aboard Air Force Two, I rolled my eyes and thought, *Here we go,* as the plane banked west to Colorado.

Arriving in Vail, we settled into our condominium and began to enjoy a meaningful holiday season together. We spent long days on the ski slopes, shared rich conversations over dinner, and relaxed around the fireplace in the evening. It was a time to focus on the gift of family and God's greatest gift that came in a manger so long ago.

As we were enjoying that time together, I later learned that many of the president's acolytes were saying that I should return to Washington. One of the president's lawyers even came to Vail requesting a meeting, likely to serve me process in a baseless lawsuit. But I stayed offline and with my family until January 2. Their presence, along with the peaceful setting, made me feel renewed once again.

As a family, we talked about the controversy but didn't dwell on it. Our kids expressed confidence in their mom and dad, knowing we would do the right thing. But they had grown up around politics, and they knew that taking a stand would come at a cost. I spoke to Charlotte on one of our lift rides up to the top of the mountain, explaining the Constitution's position on the matter. I was resolved as to what I needed to do, and the time with my family gave me an even deeper resolve. Just a few days later, I would enter the most turbulent political storm I had ever faced in politics. But we met those tumultuous days with our strength renewed because of the time we had spent together.

The Bible records that Jesus made a practice of getting away with His intimate friends. In Mark, we read how His disciples came to Him and told Him everything they had been doing and teaching. "Then, because so many people were coming and going that they did not even have a chance to eat, [Jesus] said to them, 'Come with me by yourselves to a quiet place and get some rest.' So they went away by themselves in a boat to a solitary place" (Mark 6:31–32). This aligns with God's admonition to rest throughout all of Scripture: we need to take care of ourselves, seek guidance, and value quiet to be prepared for the work ahead.

You shouldn't run away from controversy, and you must face difficulty when it comes. But spending time with the people who love you most before and after a challenging period makes a huge difference. It is good for them, and it is good for you.

When you've been through a battle or are preparing for one, get away with your family.

48

Stay

BY CHARLOTTE PENCE BOND

Therefore put on the full armor of God, so that when the day of evil comes, you may be able to stand your ground, and after you have done everything, to stand.

—EPHESIANS 6:13

In our family, we were encouraged to follow God's individual paths for our lives, to climb our own mountains, but we knew the road home and knew that the light on the front porch would be forever lit.

While I was growing up, my parents prioritized being together and supporting one another through challenges. Experiencing life united as a family means standing beside one another when the storms come. You are there for one another, you show up, but not only when it's easy. When the hard times come, you stay.

For reasons unknown to me, God has at times placed me in situations that proved to be consequential for my parents. January 6, 2021, was one of those times.

That morning, I was getting ready to go to the US Capitol for a few hours, because Mom and I knew it would be a hard, but significant, day for Dad. Later that day, he would preside over a joint session of Congress counting the electoral votes from the states for the 2020 presidential election. I planned to be there just for the beginning of the proceedings, but Mom was going to stay until it was over.

"This could be his last official duty," she told me. She was going to be there to hold his hand as he crossed the finish line, just as she has for thirty-eight years of their marriage.

As we drove to the Capitol, Dad looked outside the Secret Service limo and saw Trump supporters walking in groups, beginning to gather downtown. They cheered our motorcade, clearly thinking that he was about to do something he was not— and had made clear to the president he could not.

"They're going to be so disappointed" I heard him say softly as he looked out the window.

Mom and I gathered with a few others in Dad's ceremonial office. Soon enough, it was time for him to enter the chamber and begin the joint session to certify the election. My uncle Gregory, a congressman from Indiana, gave his little brother a hug before the day started. Once it was time to begin, all three of us went up to the gallery so we could watch. Dad called out each state, asked if there were any objections, and then moved on to the next one. It was tedious and felt like the administrative task that it was.

As we sat and watched, a member of staff approached and said we needed to return to the ceremonial office. We followed, and that was where we learned what was going on outside the Capitol. Dad arrived after us, looking visibly annoyed, because he wanted to get back to the job at hand. He's been through a few Capitol Hill lockdowns.

His lead Secret Service agent, Tim Giebels, told him that they needed to move him from the Capitol because rioters had breached the building. The ceremonial office was in a hallway with no escape—once they had reached both ends, we would be trapped—and they were already approaching one end. Dad was defiant, though. He didn't want to leave. He had no intention of giving the mob the satisfaction of seeing him run away. But as we heard people shouting from down the hall, I knew we had to do something.

Maybe Tim was hoping that my dad would budge. But I could tell he wasn't going to change his mind. They were at a standstill, and I figured there had to be a secure location inside the Capitol building that would appease both parties. I realized that if anyone with ill intentions succeeded in getting to Dad, he might be all right because he had security personnel, but the people protecting him might not be.

"Is there somewhere else we can go that's still here at the Capitol?" I asked.

"We can go to the loading dock," Tim answered.

After a short pause, Dad gave a quick nod, and the agents moved with a swiftness that marked their training. A few moments later, we were by the door, ready to go.

The agents said we needed to move quickly, and the noise outside was building. I held on to Mom's arm, planning not to let her out of my grasp. The agents opened the doors and the group surged forward, propelling us into the hallway. We headed down the route they had mapped out, and as we came to each turn, agents went in front of us to make sure it was safe.

"Clear!" we heard them call out again and again. As we turned each corner, I noticed Mom's agent covering her body with his, and I did the same, positioning myself in front of her. There was a gravity to those moments of which I was aware at the time, a realization that those agents were willing to sacrifice their own safety for the lives of our country's elected leaders—and, more broadly, for the ideals of our nation and the fundamentals it was built on.

As we made our way downstairs, I turned around to see Dad above me, walking at a steady pace, not rushing. I was annoyed that he wouldn't go faster, but true to form, he wasn't fleeing—and he certainly wasn't afraid.

When we arrived at the loading dock, we grouped together with the staff. Dad has always looked to his children for advice, support, and reactions to the events of the moment. On that day, God granted me the ability to be with him. Sometimes, when he was huddled with members of his staff, I walked up to the circle and told him what I saw happening on Twitter or listened or offered input. Other times, I stayed off at the sidelines. But I always knew I was welcome in the conversation; I knew he wanted me there.

I was in communication with my siblings, letting them know we were okay, as they told us what they were seeing unfold on television. After a while, Dad told my mom that she could head home since she had arrived at the Capitol in her own motorcade, but she wouldn't hear of it. We aren't going anywhere, she told him. If he stayed, we stayed.

I texted my cousins to let them know that Uncle Greg, their dad, was safe with us, and I sent an email to my husband, Henry, who was overseas on the USS *Nimitz* serving an extended deployment. He knew I was heading to the Capitol that day to be with Dad, so I was aware that he would wake up on the other side of the world to the news. I told him that I was in a secure location but couldn't tell him where I was. We were all aware of the need not to put our location into writing.

As the situation escalated, I made a comment about the president that I quickly regretted. "It's unforgivable," I said.

Mom gave me a look and corrected me, rightfully telling me that I was in the wrong. She was right. My faith commands me to forgive others. Colossians 3:13 says, "As the Lord has for-given you, so you also must forgive." My Savior is the one who forgives, and He has forgiven me when I didn't deserve it. In the days ahead, I would spend a lot of time thinking about that mo-ment and how difficult it was to forgive people to whom I had once been close, whom I had called my friends, but who had put my dad—my hero—at risk. But we aren't told to forgive only when it's easy. Jesus told Peter that he needed to forgive oth-ers who sinned against him "not seven times, but seventy-seven times" (Matthew 18:22). Forgiveness is not something we do once; it's meant to be a continuous and intentional choice.

At the loading dock underneath the Capitol, Dad quickly got on the phone and went to work. He called the speaker of the House and the Senate majority and minority leaders and spoke with them about what should be done. They listened to him, and they respected one another. It was an encouraging thing to see.

Hours later, we were given the all clear to return to the Sen-ate chambers. Earlier in the day, I had arranged for one of my Secret Service agents to take me back to the Vice President's Residence once I had watched some of the proceedings. One of them approached me and said that it would be difficult to take me back now that the streets were closed. But at that point, they couldn't have made me leave if they had tried.

I sat in the office watching as my siblings, Michael and Au-drey, spoke with Dad over the phone, sharing their thoughts on what he needed to say in his opening remarks before the session continued. An unknown number came up on my cell phone and I answered, knowing it was my husband calling from the ship. I reassured him that I was all right. He had seen coverage of the events on television when he had woken up and quickly tried to reach me. Months later, he would tell me that in our short conversation, I sounded the most alive that he had ever heard me. And I was. Dad had an important job to do. And our family would see to it that he finished the task at hand—no matter what. The country needed him, and he needed us.

After I finished speaking with Henry, I typed up Dad's remarks as he dictated what he had scribbled down on a piece of paper, his customary way of writing. Mom and I eventually went back to the Senate balcony as Dad prepared to head to the Senate chamber.

He walked in, and the room was silent as he took his seat. His face was more determined than I'd ever seen it before. He delivered the remarks that we, his family, had helped him prepare. We had each told him what we thought he needed to convey to the senators—and to the country. We did it together, just as we always had, just as we always will. It wouldn't have been any other way.

He received a standing ovation, something extremely uncharacteristic of the sober Senate. Senators from both parties delivered inspirational speeches about our country, and they were a true example of how public servants should act in such a moment. Although rioters tried to thwart the actions of Congress through violent means, they were unsuccessful. Our leaders did the right thing—not just Dad but others at the head of our government. Democrats and Republicans alike represented the people; they showed up and did what they had been elected to do.

Since then, the political polarization of that day has threatened to pull us apart. The attempt to use January 6 as a political weapon was disheartening, because it was a unifying day in our country, and many people seem to have forgotten that.

In the days after January 6, Dad would continue to do the right thing. He refused to let politics prevail over decency and duty. He showed me what it looks like to have honor and a steady hand, but he also demonstrated the command of Christ to "love your enemies and pray for those who persecute you" (Matthew 5:44).

The following day, Audrey and her husband, Dan, came to the Vice President's Residence so we could be together. I can vividly picture my little sister's face, a mixture of concern and relief, as she wasted no time, walked straight up to me and pulled me into a deep hug. *We were okay.*

When my dad walked Audrey and Dan out to their car at the end of the day, Audrey gave him a hug and told him, "For such a time as this."

It was a reminder that God had made him vice president for a reason, just as He had placed Esther in a position of authority to save the Jewish people (Esther 4:14).

By God's grace, we would continue to grow stronger as a family, even amid the storm. The patterns to which our family had grown accustomed over the years culminated in a moment of unity that helped Dad accomplish what he needed to do. The foundation of faith and unity my parents had built over almost four decades of marriage gave him assurance in his actions. When seemingly insurmountable pressure was brought to bear on him, when he arrived at his moment of testing, he looked around amid the chaos, and I know he was sure of at least one thing: he wasn't alone. He knew that his family was behind him and God had led us there.

Establish a foundation that will not break down when the tests arrive, and make sure it is strong enough to support your family, too.

Go together, stand together—and when the mob is at the door—stay.

Epilogue

God sets the lonely in families.

—PSALM 68:6

T hank you for joining us on this journey. We hope our family's lessons captured in the pages of *Go Home for Dinner* have made you smile. And we pray that the principles and practical advice in this book will encourage you to put faith and family first, which we believe is essential for our families, our communities, and our nation.

Today, the American family is in free fall. Marriage is on the decline, and raising children is seen as more of a burden than a blessing. People are spending less time with their loved ones, and a report by the US surgeon general announced that this country is facing an "epidemic of loneliness and isolation." Surveys reveal that around half of adults in the United States say they are lonely.[1] It's clear that families are in trouble. And when families are in trouble, America is in trouble.

The very existence of the traditional family is at risk, as marriage itself becomes less and less popular. In 2020, nearly a third of households in the United States consisted of one person, whereas in 1940 fewer than one in ten American homes were made up of just one person.[2] A study by the National Center for Family and Marriage Research found that the marriage rate has dropped by nearly 60 percent since the 1970s.[3,4] A 2023 Pew Research Center report found that parents are more concerned about their children's careers and financial future than they are about their having a family of their own.[5] Eighty-eight percent of respondents said it was "extremely or very important to them that their children be financially independent" or have a job they enjoy, but only around 20 percent said the same about their kids getting married or having children.

It seems that we've lost our sense of self as a nation precisely because we've lost our sense of family. The family is considered to be merely one component of our busy social and professional lives, but the truth is, it is the core. It is the underpinning of all we can hope to accomplish, and it doesn't effortlessly become stable and secure. It must be cultivated, and it's up to you to do it. The Bible is clear on the importance of marriage: "Husbands, love your wives," a wife should "respect her husband" (Ephesians 5:25, 33), "train up a child in the way he should go" (Proverbs 22:6), and "manage [your] own family well" (1 Timothy 3:4) are some of the highlights. God wants our marriages and our families to be our priority. And I believe when we make His priorities our priorities, we are blessed.

But in the twenty-first century, too many Americans look to popular culture or government to support their families instead of taking on the task themselves. Throughout my career in public life, I have stood behind incentives in laws that support the family, whether through supporting traditional marriage, ending the marriage penalty tax, promoting pro-adoption legislation, or providing paid family leave to federal employees. Initiatives such as these benefit families, but ultimately, no government program will ever replace the power and impact of the individual American family. Our country's standing on the world stage and its economic might are not built on the strength of its politics. The destiny of America is in the hands of the American people, and the strength of America is ultimately grounded in the strength of the American family.

In 1790, the Irish philosopher Edmund Burke wrote, "To love the little platoon we belong to in society, is the first principle . . . of public affections. It is the first link in the series by which we proceed toward a love to our country and to mankind."[6] The family is the first "little platoon" to which we belong. It is the focal point that determines how we understand the world and orient ourselves to our part in it.

Democracy depends on heavy doses of civility, but today our civil discourse has weakened as Americans are losing the art of discussing issues with one another. Our divisive politics is not just contributing to our lack of connection; it is a result of it. We are not coming together where it is most necessary, and we are seeing the consequences. There is a tradition we have put to the side, a place we have let gather dust: the dinner table.

Across the dinner table, you are taught manners and mutual respect. You learn how to wait your turn and share with others. You celebrate your culture and the culture of others. As we know from personal experience, families are not monolithic and are made up of diverse viewpoints. American families are spending less time with one another, which has likely led to a deterioration in our ability to disagree respectfully. From 2003 to 2020, time spent socializing with family members in a household went down by five hours per month, and social isolation rose by twenty-four hours per month.[7]

Russell Kirk, in his *Concise Guide to Conservatism*, discussed the conservative's understanding of the family. Kirk knew that family was—and is—the heartbeat of our nation. Without it, our country cannot thrive, and it may not survive at all. "The conservative knows that, the family lacking, nothing very important in our culture can be preserved or improved," he wrote. "The traditional family . . . gives us those roots without which we all would be just so many lonely little atoms of humanity, unprincipled and at the mercy of some iron political domination."[8]

The breakdown of the family is also the precursor of the growth of tyranny. As Americans, we are beginning to see this happen, and we should be concerned. Our lack of connectedness has led to a dearth of core beliefs, an increase in isolation, and an erosion of liberties and American values. Kirk quoted Robert Nisbet, who wrote about how authoritarian regimes and totalitarians have always seen strong families as a threat: "The shrewd totalitarian mentality knows well the powers of intimate kinship and religious devotion for keeping alive in a population values and incentives which might well, in the future, serve as the basis of resistance. Thus to emancipate each member, and especially the younger members, from the family was an absolute necessity."[9]

So a strong family isn't just a nice idea; it is the first step in returning this country to its core values, which, grounded in faith, are the bedrock of our nation. We look too often to politicians to fix what is plaguing our country, but to bring America back to the fullness of strength that saw us through our revolution, a civil war, a depression, and two world wars, we must look closer to home. If you want a stronger America, first strengthen your own home. If you, like many Americans, are wondering what you can do to get our country back on a path of prosperity and give it a brighter future, put your family first. If you want to help America, go home for dinner.

As you can tell from the pages of this book, for us, everything begins with faith, because, as the Bible promises, "God sets the lonely in families" (Psalm 68:6). When we fix our eyes on the author of faith and family, we will find the grace to be the husband, wife, and parents that He called us to be.

Jesus said, "I stand at the door and knock. If anyone hears my voice and opens the door, I will come in and eat with that person, and they with me" (Revelation 3:20). He wants to come to your table. If you have not yet done so, with gentleness and respect, we encourage you to invite Him to come into your heart, to lead you every day, and you will experience the deep richness and peace that comes when you choose to follow Him.

It may not come on a hillside in the rain or after time spent abroad, but "If you confess with your mouth that Jesus is Lord and believe in your heart that God raised him from the dead, you will be saved" (Romans 10:9).

Your life will never be the same. Your family will be better for it, and our nation will be strengthened.

President Ronald Reagan said in his Farewell Address to the Nation on January 11, 1989, "And let me offer lesson number one about America: All great change in America begins at the dinner table. So, tomorrow night in the kitchen I hope the talking begins."[10]

So do we.

Be a parent who listens, follow your peace, return to the rock, build levees around your marriage, and teach your kids to speak their dreams. Give your family Sunday, carry your children, sit awhile with Him every day, and have a family night. Trust God, chase your dreams, and when you do, go together.

As our family embarks on another journey to serve our country, it should be clear that we have no other view than this: the ultimate cure for what ails America will be found not in the boardrooms of this country or the halls of government but at the dinner table, where our faith and family are renewed.

We hope that these tools will be a blessing to you and our gentle advice will encourage you to think about what you can do to strengthen your family. Our prayer is that the words of this book may in some way encourage the ancient admonition to "turn the hearts of the parents to their children, and the hearts of the children to their parents" (Malachi 4:6). But the words included in these pages are meant to be a call to our country, as well. America is being tested. Whether or not freedom prevails will be determined by the faith and families of America. And therein lies our hope.

As more Americans put faith and family first, we know the best days for the greatest nation on Earth are yet to come.

Save your family. Save America. *Go home for dinner.*

Mike Pence
Charlotte Pence Bond
July 2023
Zionsville, Indiana

Notes

PREFACE

1. "Normandy American Cemetery," American Battle Monuments Commission, https://www.abmc.gov/normandy.
2. Erica Pandey, "America the Single," Axios, February 25, 2023, https://www.axios.com/2023/02/25/marriage-declining-single-dating-taxes-relationships.

1: GO HOME FOR DINNER

1. Robert J. Waldinger and Marc S. Schulz, *The Good Life: Lessons from the World's Longest Scientific Study of Happiness* (New York: Simon & Schuster, 2023), 221.

3: FULFILL YOUR PURPOSE

1. Emphasis added.

4: EMBRACE FAITH

1. Henry David Thoreau, *Walden: Reflections of the Simple Living in Natural Surroundings*, American Classics Series (e-artnow, 2017), Kindle.

6: TALK FAITH FIRST

1. "Read the Bible in a Year—August 2016," The Billy Graham Library, August 1, 2016, https://billygrahamlibrary.org/read-the-bible-in-a-year-august-2016/.

2. Bethany Verrett, "What Does 'Helpmate' Really Mean in Marriage?," Bible Study Tools, December 16, 2022, https://www.biblestudytools.com/bible-study/topical-studies/what-does-helpmate-really-mean-in-marriage.html.

7: GO TO THE SHOOT

1. William D. Dalton, "Hinkle Fieldhouse," Encyclopedia of Indianapolis, February 2021. https://indyencyclopedia.org/hinkle-fieldhouse/.

2. Dana Hunsinger Benbow, "Finally, an Image of Bobby Plump's Winning Shot," *IndyStar*, September 13, 2016, https://www.indystar.com/story/sports/high-school/2016/9/12/missing-photo-bobby-plumps-winning-shot/89979940/.

3. Jennifer Gunnels, "The History of Hinkle Fieldhouse," Butler Stories, March 15, 2021, https://stories.butler.edu/the-history-of-hinkle-fieldhouse/.

4. Chris Nashawaty, "34 Years Ago, *Hoosiers* Was the Underdog Movie About Underdogs That No One Expected to Succeed," *Esquire*, November 14, 2020, https://www.esquire.com/entertainment/movies/a34673344/hoosiers-anniversary-essay-story-making-of-analysis/.

5. Gare Joyce, "'We Got a Memo About a Movie . . . ,'" ESPN, November 16, 2010, https://www.espn.com/espn/news/story?id=5813889.

6. svonhaney, "Checking the Dimensions at Butler.avi," YouTube, March 15, 2010, https://www.youtube.com/watch?v=mb4QP6kNAoc.

8: HAVE THE FAITH OF A HUMMINGBIRD

1. Associated Press, "Motherhood Deferred: U.S. Median Age for Giving Birth Hits 30," NBC News, May 8, 2022, https://www.nbcnews.com/news/motherhood-deferred-us-median-age-giving-birth-hits-30-rcna27827.

2. Anne Morse, "Stable Fertility Rates 1990–2019 Mask Distinct

Variations by Age," United States Census Bureau, April 6, 2022, https://www.census.gov/library/stories/2022/04/fertility-rates-declined-for-younger-women-increased-for-older-women.html.

3. Jackie Wilson, "(Your Love Keeps Liftin' Me) Higher and Higher," Genius, https://genius.com/Jackie-wilson-your-love-keeps-liftin-me-higher-and-higher-lyrics.

4. "How Many Couples Are Waiting to Adopt a Baby?," American Adoptions, https://www.americanadoptions.com/pregnant/waiting_adoptive_families.

5. Jeff Diamant and Besheer Mohamed, "What the Data Says About Abortion in the U.S.," Pew Research Center, January 11, 2023, https://www.pewresearch.org/short-reads/2023/01/11/what-the-data-says-about-abortion-in-the-u-s-2/.

10: KNOW YOU ARE NEVER BETTER

1. Stephen R. Covey, *The 7 Habits of Highly Effective People* (New York: Free Press, 1990).

2. "Volunteer," Theodore Roosevelt Birthplace, National Park Service, https://www.nps.gov/thrb/getinvolved/volunteer.htm?fullweb=1.

11: KNOW THAT CHILDREN HEAL YOUR HEART

1. "Brief History of the Five Stages of Grief," Grief.com, https://grief.com/history-of-grief/.

17: FOLLOW YOUR PEACE

1. BST and Crosswalk Staff, "The Bible Story of Gideon," Biblestudytools.com, September 28, 2022, www.biblestudytools.com/bible-stories/the-bible-story-of-gideon.html.

18: GO TOGETHER

1. Maureen Groppe, Chelsea Schneider, and Tony Cook, "Pence Says He Can't Defend Trump's Comments," *IndyStar*, October 8, 2016, https://www.indystar.com/story/news/politics/2016/10/08/pence-says-he-cant-defend-trumps-comments/91786874/.

2. "Watts, Julius Caesar, Jr. (J. C.)," History, Art & Archives, United States House of Representatives, https://history.house.gov/People /Detail/23468.

19: BUILD LEVEES

1. Nikita Vladimirov, "Trump: Pence Has 'One Hell of a Good Marriage,'" *The Hill*, March 31, 2017, https://thehill.com/blogs/blog -briefing-room/news/326814-trump-pence-has-one-hell-of-a -good-marriage/.
2. Ashley Parker, "Karen Pence Is the Vice President's 'Prayer Warrior,' Gut Check and Shield," *Washington Post*, March 28, 2017, https:// www.washingtonpost.com/politics/karen-pence-is-the-vice-pres idents-prayer-warrior-gut-check-and-shield/2017/03/28/3d7a26ce -0a01-11e7-8884-96e6a6713f4b_story. html.
3. Maureen Groppe, Chelsea Schneider, and Tony Cook, "Pence Says He Can't Defend Trump's Comments," *IndyStar*, October 8, 2016, https:// www.indystar.com/story/news/politics/2016/10/08/pence-says-he -cant-defend-trumps-comments/91786874/.

20: FIND THE LIZARD

1. "Your Bearded Dragon Likes to Watch TV—and Other Friendly Facts About Beardies," Long Island Bird & Exotics Veterinary Clinic, March 19, 2023, https://www.birdexoticsvet.com/post/2019/02/14 /your-bearded-dragon-likes-to-watch-tv-and-other-friendly-facts -about-beardies.

21: LET MUSIC MINISTER TO YOU

1. *Merriam-Webster*, "encourage (*v.*)," www.merriam-webster.com/dic tionary/encourage.
2. Amy Grant, "All I Ever Have to Be," Genius, https://genius.com/Amy -grant-all-i-ever-have-to-be-lyrics.
3. Casting Crowns, "Voice of Truth," Genius, https://genius.com/Casting -crowns-voice-of-truth-lyrics.

4. Michael W. Smith, "Above All," Lyrics.com, https://www.lyrics.com
/lyric/5063615/Michael+W.+Smith/Above+All.

5. Steven Curtis Chapman, "Glorious Unfolding," Lyrics.com, https://
www.lyrics.com/lyric/29691964/Steven+Curtis+Chapman/Glorious
+Unfolding.

24: TAKE TIME TO PAY YOUR RESPECTS

1. "Abraham Lincoln," The White House, https://www.whitehouse.gov
/about-the-white-house/presidents/abraham-lincoln/.

2. William E. Bartelt, *There I Grew Up: Remembering Abraham Lincoln's
Indiana Youth* (Indianapolis: Indiana Historical Society Press, 2008).

3. "'There I Grew Up . . .' A. Lincoln," Lincoln Boyhood National Memorial, Indiana, National Park Service, https://www.nps.gov/libo/index
.htm.

4. Spencer County Visitors Bureau, "Lincoln's Indiana Boyhood Home,"
Santa Claus, Indiana, https://santaclausind.org/play/lincoln.

5. "Nancy Hanks Lincoln," National Park Service, https://www.nps.gov
/people/nancy-hanks-lincoln.htm.

6. Christopher Klein, "The Two Mothers Who Molded Lincoln," History.com, March 29, 2023, https://www.history.com/news/the-two
-mothers-who-molded-lincoln.

7. Doug Wead, *The Raising of a President: The Mothers and Fathers of
Our Nation's Leaders* (New York: Atria Books, 2005), Kindle.

8. Jill York O'Bright, *There I Grew Up: A History of the Administration of
Abraham Lincoln's Boyhood Home* (Ann Arbor: University of Michigan Library, 1987), 184.

9. "Plymouth Notch, Vermont," The Center for Land Use Interpretation,
https://clui.org/ludb/site/plymouth-notch.

10. "Calvin Coolidge Takes the Oath of Office by the Light of a Kerosene
Lamp," New England Historical Society, https://newenglandhistorical
society.com/calvin-coolidge-takes-oath-of-office-light-kerosene-lamp/.

11. "Madison Family Cemetery at Madison's Montpelier Estate," The History List, https://www.thehistorylist.com/sites/madison-family-cem

etery-at-madison-s-montpelier-estate-montpelier-station-virginia
/list-of-presidential-graves-roadtrip-to-their-gravesites-burial-places
-historic-sites-and-homes.

26: RETURN TO THE ROCK

1. "Vice President's Swearing-in Ceremony," Joint Congressional Committee on Inaugural Ceremonies, https://www.inaugural.senate.gov /vice-presidents-swearing-in-ceremony/.

27: FACE TRAGEDY TOGETHER

1. Pat Bauer, "American Airlines Flight 77," Encyclopaedia Britannica, https://www.britannica.com/event/American-Airlines-flight-77.
2. "The Attack on the Pentagon," Naval History and Heritage Command, https://www.history.navy.mil/research/archives/digital-exhibits -highlights/photo-galleries-9-11/pentagon-attack.html.
3. "Thomas J. Ridge, Secretary of Homeland Security 2003–2005," U.S. Department of Homeland Security, https://www.dhs.gov/thomas-j -ridge.

28: ENCOURAGE ONE ANOTHER

1. Adam Smith, *The Wealth of Nations*, Bibliomania, http://www.biblio mania.com/2/1/65/112/frameset.html.

30: WHEN YOU'RE THERE, BE THERE

1. Simon Romero, "The Right Connections; The Simple BlackBerry Allowed Contact When Phones Failed," *New York Times*, September 20, 2001, https://www.nytimes.com/2001/09/20/technology/the-right-con nections-the-simple-blackberry-allowed-contact-when-phones-failed .html.
2. Reuters Staff, "Timeline: Change at the Top of Research in Motion," Reuters, January 22, 2012, https://www.reuters.com/article/us-rim -timeline/timeline-change-at-the-top-of-research-in-motion-idUS TRE80M05120120123.
3. Daniel Libit, "Are Members BlackBerry Addicts?," Politico, June 11,

2008, https://www.politico.com/story/2008/06/are-members-black
berry-addicts-010995.

4. *Hearing on Security Updates Since September 11, 2001, Hearing Before the Committee on House Administration, House of Representatives,* 107th Cong. (September 10, 2002), https://www.govinfo.gov
/content/pkg/CHRG-107hhrg82351/html/CHRG-107hhrg82351.htm/.

34: CARRY YOUR CHILDREN

1. Sam Opsahl, "Brickyard 200," Encyclopedia of Indianapolis, February
2021, https://indyencyclopedia.org/brickyard-400/.

2. "Indianapolis Motor Speedway Museum," Indianapolis Motor Speedway,
https://www.indianapolismotorspeedway.com/at-the-track/museum.

3. "Indianapolis Motor Speedway," Wikipedia, https://en.wikipedia.org
/wiki/Indianapolis_Motor_Speedway.

4. "On This Day in 1994: Jeff Gordon Wins the Inaugural Brickyard 400," Fox News, August 6, 2016, https://www.foxnews.com
/sports/on-this-day-in-1994-jeff-gordon-wins-the-inaugural-brick
yard-400.

5. Indianapolis Motor Speedway, "Jeff Gordon Wins Inaugural 1994
Brickyard 400 at IMS," YouTube, July 11, 2018, https://www.youtube
.com/watch?v=kepED76mIdA.

37: TRAIN TOGETHER

1. "Marine Corps Marathon," My Best Runs, https://mybestruns.com
/MarineCorpsMarathon.

2. "New Way to Beat the Bridge," Marine Corps Marathon, August 17, 2018,
https://www.marinemarathon.com/new-way-to-beat-the-bridge/.

39: FOLLOW YOUR INSTINCT TO SERVE

1. Kevin DeYoung, "What Makes Jesus Marvel?," The Gospel Coalition,
May 21, 2010, https://www.thegospelcoalition.org/blogs/kevin-de
young/what-makes-jesus-marvel/.

2. *Merriam-Webster,* "centurion (*n.*)," https://www.merriam-webster
.com/dictionary/centurion.

3. "The Gettysburg Address," Abraham Lincoln Online, https://www .abrahamlincolnonline.org/lincoln/speeches/gettysburg.htm.

45: WHEN YOU'RE BEING HONORED, HONOR YOUR FAMILY

1. Joe Williams, "(Back Home Again in) Indiana," Lyrics.com, https:// www.lyrics.com/lyric/1081998/Joe+Williams/%28Back+Home +Again+In%29+Indiana.

47: GET AWAY WITH FAMILY

1. "Acropolis," History.com, June 29, 2023, https://www.history.com /topics/ancient-greece/acropolis.

EPILOGUE

1. *Our Epidemic of Loneliness and Isolation 2023: The U.S. Surgeon General's Advisory on the Healing Effects of Social Connection and Community*, Office of the U.S. Surgeon General, https://www.hhs.gov/sites /default/files/surgeon-general-social-connection-advisory.pdf.

2. Lydia Anderson et al., "Home Alone: More Than a Quarter of All Households Have One Person," United States Census Bureau, June 8, 2023, https://www.census.gov/library/stories/2023/06/more-than-a -quarter-all-households-have-one-person.html.

3. Julissa Cruz, *Marriage: More Than a Century of Change* (Bowling Green, OH: National Center for Family & Marriage Research, 2013), https://www.bgsu.edu/content/dam/BGSU/college-of-arts-and-sci ences/NCFMR/documents/FP/FP-13-13.pdf.

4. "Provisional Number of Marriages and Marriage Rate: United States, 2000–2021," National Center for Health Statistics, Centers for Disease Control and Prevention, https://www.cdc.gov/nchs/data/dvs/mar riage-divorce/national-marriage-divorce-rates-00-21.pdf.

5. Rachel Minkin and Juliana Menasce Horowitz, "Parenting in America Today," Pew Research Center, January 24, 2023, https://www.pew research.org/social-trends/2023/01/24/parenting-in-america-today/.

6. Edmund Burke, *Reflections on the Revolution in France*, (Hamilton,

Ontario: McMaster University), https://socialsciences.mcmaster.ca/e con/ugcm/3ll3/burke/revfrance.pdf, 39.

7. *Our Epidemic of Loneliness and Isolation 2023.*

8. Russell Kirk, *Concise Guide to Conservatism* (Washington, DC: Regnery Gateway, 2019), 38.

9. Robert Nisbet, *The Quest for Community: A Study in the Ethics of Order and Freedom* (Washington, DC: Regnery Gateway, 2010), Kindle.

10. Ronald Reagan, "Farewell Address to the Nation," January 11, 1989, Ronald Reagan Presidential Foundation & Institute, https://www.reaganfoundation.org/media/128652/farewell.pdf.

About the Authors

MIKE PENCE served as the forty-eighth Vice President of the United States (2017–2021), as the fiftieth Governor of Indiana (2013–2017), and as a member of the US House of Representatives (2001–2013).

CHARLOTTE PENCE BOND is a bestselling author and the daughter of former Vice President Mike Pence and Second Lady Karen Pence. She is a proud Navy spouse, mother, and the author of *Where You Go: Life Lessons from My Father*, as well as the Marlon Bundo children's series, which her mother illustrated. She works as a contributor at *The Daily Wire*, and is passionate about the pro-life movement.